GARY MOORE is a Senior Vice President of Investments in the Tampa, Florida, office of one of America's largest investment firms. He and a few associates have joined to form the Social Investment Group to assist those seeking a commonsense, long-term approach to responsible investing. Basic estate and gift planning are also a focus of the group.

He is a member of the Social Investment Forum, the Council on Economic Priorities, and the Christian Stewardship Association. He and his wife, Sherry, are co-founders of the Institute for Thoughtful Investing. The Institute is an informal group of financial professionals who study, lecture, and write about those individuals and institutions, both religious and financial, that apply the Judeo-Christian ethic to the modern handling of wealth. In his spare moments, he is studying for ordination.

Jesus did not speak directly against wealth and money lending, but he did emphasize the dangers of riches and the rich man's responsibility for the poor. Evidently, the continuing test of the capitalist is the priority of his love and the purpose of his riches.

The question for the future is whether [an economy such as America's] can retain the value of individual freedom while recapturing the sense of social responsibility. Evangelical Christianity has a stake in that question because it is a moral issue with implications for the future of the church.

Baker's Dictionary of Christian Ethics

THE THOUGHTFUL CHRISTIAN'S GUIDE TO INVESTING

Gary D. Moore

Zondervan Books
Zondervan Publishing House
Grand Rapids, Michigan

THE THOUGHTFUL CHRISTIAN'S GUIDE TO INVESTING

Copyright © 1990 by Gary D. Moore

Zondervan Books are published by
Zondervan Publishing House
1415 Lake Drive, S.E.
Grand Rapids, MI 49506

Library of Congress Cataloging-in-Publication Data

Moore, Gary D.
  The thoughtful Christian's guide to investing / Gary D. Moore.
     p.   cm.
  ISBN 0-310-53131-4
  1. Finance, Personal— Religious aspects— Christianity.
I. Title.
HG179.M615 1990
332.029'2— dc20   90-33155
                                                   CIP

Printed in the United States of America

 90 91 92 93 94 95 96 / CH / 10 9 8 7 6 5 4 3 2

To my parents, *who indicated the proper roads of life to me;* **to my wife**, *who has suffered the occasional detours; and* **to my son** *— may his generation travel roads burdened by fewer tolls.*

Contents

Investment information is general in nature and should be discussed with competent counsel or seriously researched before use. Your financial situation is unique and each investment must be considered as it pertains to your particular financial picture. This text is solely the opinion of the author and should not be considered the opinion of any business or religious organization with which he might be affiliated.

To eliminate the need for the annoying repetition of qualifiers such as "usually," "normally," and "generally," the reader should understand that I am speaking of the norm. There are ALWAYS exceptions to EVERYTHING.

Acknowledgments

There are so many people who made this book possible that I will simply mention those directly involved.

Fred Osborn, Planned Giving Officer of the Episcopal Church, first thought this book might be of use to more people than those in my local area. The Reverend Jim Bingham first thought it might be of sufficient interest to actually publish on a commercial basis. The Reverend Doctor John Santosuosso—being a professor, author, clergyman, and surprisingly knowledgeable investor—was uniquely qualified to review this type of work. His approval comforted me as I explored some areas in which I had limited expertise.

The talents of Judith Markham, my editor, are well-respected—even legendary—in the publishing world. My limited writing skills and our diverse subject matter presented enormous challenges in sharing my thoughts. It's a tribute to Judith's abilities that you will never know just how enormous! It has been a great joy and a rare privilege to work with one so talented.

And finally, I would like to thank John Templeton. There were times during the mid-1980s when it seemed to me that few people who handled money were seriously concerned with Christian principles. His books about ethical business practices and the magnificent capabilities of our God assured me that it only seemed that way. The seminary he established, his Prize for Progress in Religion, and his prudent management of money for over 600,000 investors proved to me that God and our modern uses of money are not poles apart, never to be brought together. And his endorsement of this book played a critical role in assuring others that there might be some legitimacy in the work of this unknown person.

I am deeply grateful for this gentleman's way of life, his investment philosophies, and his most gracious assistance. Wall Street and our banking institutions have been identified with less than admirable people during the 1980s. May they be identified with people such as John Templeton during the 1990s.

Foreword

ANY UNDERSTANDING of stewardship which is simply defined in terms of our giving falls far short of the Christian's responsible use of God-given assets. Jesus states the principle clearly in his parable about the nobleman and his servants to whom he gave gifts. "Put this money to work," he said, "until I come back" (Luke 19:13 NIV).

Paul enlarges on the concept when he tells us, "Now it is required that those who have been given a trust must prove faithful" (1 Cor. 4:2 NIV).

Both Jesus' words and those of Paul remind us that there must be thoughtful, careful management and investing of our resources. Unfortunately, many of us have not seen how, in the materialistic society of our day, we can be effective and faithful in the use of our money. Can we be honoring to God, faithful to ourselves and our families, and ethically and morally responsible in relation to our society?

Gary Moore shows the way to lead us from the biblical context, through church history, and into our highly charged, investment-dominated society. At this point, lacking his background and insights, many of us have floundered. Here is where he comes to our aid with careful, sound, and prudent insights that will indeed help us to be obedient to our Lord and responsible in our world.

Edward J. Hales
Executive Director
Christian Stewardship Association

OFTEN A FALSE DICHOTOMY underlies books that deal with our Christian faith and the matter of money. The assumed dichotomy is that Christian faith is a spiritual matter and money is worldly. In this false dichotomy, the two must be kept separate, lest our faith be tainted by filthy lucre. Gary Moore's work faces this dilemma squarely and integrates the subject of money with Christian faith. The Bible makes it clear that they are inextricably linked. Moore does not shrink from this reality.

In addition to its holistic approach to the subject of investment, this book is a compendium of guidelines and principles to help the thoughtful Christian struggling to make investment decisions. Help is provided for adult investors of all ages. The listing of principles of investing is especially worth noting.

At the same time, the book deals genuinely and compassionately with ethical issues and the welfare of fellow humans. Indeed, the social conscience revealed in Moore's comments is touching. Nor is the timely subject of environmental concerns overlooked as part of Christian stewardship.

As we enter the decade of the 1990s and approach the 21st century, this book will be of genuine help to the thoughtful and caring Christian.

Ronald E. Vallet
National Council of Churches
Commission on Stewardship
New York, NY

Introduction

THERE ARE MANY BOOKS available on the subject of money: how to earn it, how to save it, how to manage it, how to spend it. And there are a number of books that deal with money and the Christian faith. Several of these are excellent resources and provide helpful insights, but for me they have provided only partial answers.

For example, some of them say that Christians can't have money and be faithful too. But is the abandonment of money to non-Christians the only viable approach to the world's problems? Whether we like it or not, money is vital in making our world go round. And since it is, shouldn't Christians try to affect the way it goes round by having something to say about the way money is used?

Some Christian authors say that God will provide and that we shouldn't concern ourselves with money. But I simply cannot believe in a welfare faith. The Bible does teach that God will provide for our needs, but it also teaches that we have been given the power of choice as part of that provision. God may provide us with "manna" each day, but we must go out and gather that manna. God may lead us to the land of milk and honey, but we must walk the difficult road that leads there, and we must take possession of the land. We have to follow directions, walk on our own two feet as God enables us, and help our needy brothers and sisters along the way. The Almighty has always helped those who help themselves, but has always blessed those who help others.

Some books maintain that we should be good stewards and allow God to control our money. This is a sentiment I respect and is the essence of my own philosophy. But exactly what does it mean to be a good steward? Simply mouthing the phrase is not enough. Blind imitation diverts us from taking personal responsibility to search for the financial tools to accomplish God's work in a changing world.

I will not pretend to know what approach God prefers for us to take in handling money, for there often seem to be conflicting paths available. Genesis 47:20–26 says that because of the severe famine in Egypt, Joseph was able to buy up all the land for the king. Does this mean that government should control the wealth? The testimonies of a number of devout American businesspeople who earn, manage, and give their wealth generously to the service of God and humanity encourage me to believe that they have captured the essence of faith by putting individual wealth to such use. Then I read the peaceful words of Mother Teresa who describes the perfect security system as "owning nothing anyone would steal," and I believe she has unlocked the door of faith. What I do know, without doubt, is that we should not be tempted, as I once was, to believe that the Bible says nothing on the subject. It simply says everything on the subject. I expect, in humbler moments, even economists would admit that God could make any economic system work fairly well. So while I am totally uncertain about whether "responsible capitalism" is the ultimate desire of God, I am equally certain it is a step in the right direction. I will simply be bold enough to point out that in order to get the Ten Commandments from the hand of the Almighty, Moses had to work his way up the mountain and get terribly close to his God. Then he shook the status quo up a bit.

Some books by Christian financial planners take this more practical approach. They quote Scripture about the merits of money and investing. They speak of the importance of the tithe and recommend that we avoid greed, debt, and speculation. These are very good messages of course, but they are a little like telling someone to avoid sin. Avoiding sin is an important first step for Christians, but it also can be simply a neutral step. Just because you aren't harming your neighbors doesn't mean you are necessarily doing anything to help them. If we are to mature as believers, we must actively pursue good works. A Christian sense of time, neighbor, and purpose will ultimately accomplish those works.

Although I have given some brief definitions and explanations of financial terms and vocabulary throughout this book and have included many practical helps in the Resource Center in the last section, I am not spending a great deal of time with questions like "What is a stock?" or "What is a bond?" There are a hundred sources and a hundred people that can readily supply that information. Also, I tend to avoid getting too technical, because if there ever was an area where "a little knowledge is a dangerous thing," it is the area of investing. I have counseled dozens of people who went to an "investment course" at a local hotel. Armed with "knowledge" and confidence, they then went out and bought all the wrong investments at all the wrong times.

While a basic working vocabulary is helpful, what you really need is to know how to think about investments and how to use them. And you particularly need to understand the impact that various investments will have not only on yourself, but on your neighbor and the world around you.

My goal in this book is to help you avoid creating financial problems for yourself and society by the way you invest your money; to avoid paying counselors such as banks, brokers, and money managers to create those problems with your money; and to avoid entrusting your money to those who will create problems with it by using it for their own short-term benefit. And I will try to provide prudent alternatives to the areas I am personally concerned about, since discussing problems without discussing solutions can lead to cynicism. America has enough of that today to disable our financial system.

Most of my Christian clients who invest through the public markets think I'm kidding when I ask, "Have you considered investing for the good of humanity?"

Perhaps you too see images of endless charity when you hear that question. If so, I challenge you to apply the teachings of your faith. Living out your faith will strengthen every area of your life, including how you invest your money.

Part 1

LAYING THE
FOUNDATION

1

Getting Started

The heart of man is of a larger mold: it can at once comprise a taste for the possessions of earth and the love of those of heaven; at times it may seem to cling devotedly to the one, but it will never be long without thinking of the other.

Alexis de Tocqueville

FEW SYMBOLS IN AMERICA are as identified with wealth, power, and financial security as Wall Street. From Monday through Friday the Street channels an incalculable amount of money in various directions through its investment firms and banks, which in turn wield awesome power—a power far greater than most of us realize. Power to change the nature of great corporations, governmental authorities, and the ownership of our earth's natural resources. Investments from the Street provide retirement benefits for millions who have never even visited an investment firm or entered the brokerage division of their bank. But along with this money and power comes greed, and the financial security usually associated with investments can quickly turn to anxiety during periods like October of 1987.

About two years ago the "wall" of Wall Street became very real to me. Prior to that I had placed my faith in institutions, government, and human knowledge. I had worked my way up to become a senior vice-president of a major Wall Street investment firm. I faithfully read *The Wall Street Journal*, *Money*, *Forbes*, *Barrons*, a dozen financial publications, and stock reports by the thousands.

So when I ran into the wall, my faith in myself and my investments made my collision even harder. I had traveled the world with investment companies, counseled hundreds of investors about their financial concerns, and felt that I thoroughly understood the financial world. Suddenly, through my own personal experience and my counseling of those who seemed to have "everything," I began to realize that money, upward mobility, and the other elements of the Great American Dream were unable to provide true security and happiness. I was reasonably successful in making money and helping others to do so, but I didn't have peace about it.

I had invested my own money in the classic "investment pyramid" style, where you begin with conservative investments and add higher-risk, higher-return ventures as you accumulate more money. Within ten years I had reached the top of the pyramid and had begun putting smaller amounts of money in commodities and speculative real estate. As long as they looked promising, I considered most investments.

But along the way I was also learning two valuable, but expensive lessons. First, I learned that moving from prudent, conservative investing toward the high-risk, high-return at the top of the chart had actually drastically reduced the return on my money—not to mention the return *of* my money. And second, I discovered that many of these investments gave me an uncomfortable feeling, even though they promised high returns.

Another factor that entered the picture was the birth of my son in 1986, which prompted me to begin considering those around me more fully when I made investing decisions. This deeper consideration and my top-of-the-pyramid speculation seemed in conflict.

Early in 1987 I began reading disturbing reports about the health of the government agencies that insured my certificates of deposit. The Federal Savings and Loan Insurance Corporation (FSLIC) looked almost dead, and the Federal Deposit Insurance Corporation (FDIC) seemed to be getting weaker by the moment. Every day another banking institution closed its doors.

Then October arrived, and I completely forgot about those worries. The stock market crashed and killed an old friend I'd "listened to" for a long time, E. F. Hutton. Suddenly forced mergers and layoffs swept Wall Street.

No one had predicted this disaster, and I found I was losing faith in myself, in other "experts," in financial institutions, and even in the government itself. I didn't know what to do with money; yet my entire livelihood

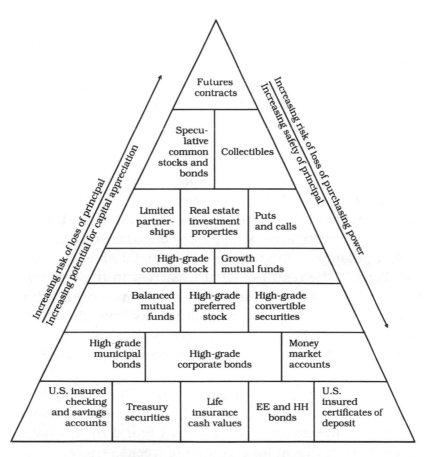

Investment Vehicle Pyramid

depended on knowing what to do with money. Only when you find yourself plunged into this kind of sea of despair, drowning in information but grasping for bits of wisdom, do you begin to understand the true meaning of "futility." Confusion and stress began taking their toll. Other people were going through similar turmoil, of course, but they continued to look to brokers, bankers, *The Wall Street Journal* and *Money* magazine. I had already tried that, so I knew I had to look elsewhere.

My first instinct was to quit my job—not an unusual reaction. When people break their self-absorption long enough to peer through the chaos around them, odds are good that they'll eventually focus on the Infinite, which is guaranteed to change their perspective of time and their world. For that reason, seminary appealed to me. Besides, I had always felt that the ministry was the highest calling this world offers the believer. But as I contemplated this move, I realized that if we all needed to be members of the clergy to find the answers to life's problems, then my faith was pretty irrelevant. Also, I was good at what I did and felt it was a vocation God had given me. If my faith was valid at all, it had to be relevant for every area of life, including the financial.

So I broadened my search for financial answers, and this book is the result of what I learned in the first two years of that quest. Initially I began writing this material down to help me organize my own thoughts, but gradually I began to wonder if perhaps what I was learning might help others struggling with the same issues and questions.

The Bible says, "Teach a child how he should live, and he will remember it all his life" (Prov. 22:6). Now I discovered the meaning of that as I found myself back on my parents' farm for a couple of weeks, studying the Bible and stewardship writings for reassurance and answers. One of the most important things I discovered was that God didn't want just 10% of my money; God wanted 100% of it.

God doesn't want just 10% of our money; God wants 100% of it.

I also discovered that I could have avoided 90% of my investing mistakes over the years if I had spent a little more of my time reading Proverbs, Ecclesiastes, Luke, and James. The first two books are often credited to the wisdom of Solomon, a man who learned a lot about money the hard way. It's been estimated that he had a yearly income of over $20,000,000, and few people have studied the capabilities and futilities of wealth as thoroughly as he did. Proverbs and Ecclesiastes not only provide wise, perceptive, assuring, and frank guidelines on the subject, but also prove that God addressed the subject of money and security very early on in the history of the faith. Consider just these few examples:

"Whoever listens to me will have security. He will be safe, with no reason to be afraid" (Prov. 1:33).

"Righteous men keep their wealth, but wicked men lose theirs when hard times come" (Prov. 15:6 NIV).

"The more easily you get your wealth, the less good it will do you" (Prov. 20:21).

"Honest people will lead a full, happy life. But if you are in a hurry to get rich, you are going to be punished" (Prov. 28:20).

"If you love money, you will never be satisfied; if you long to be rich, you will never get all you want. It is useless. The richer you are, the more mouths you have to feed. All you gain is the knowledge that you are rich. A working man may or may not have enough to eat, but at least he can get a good night's sleep. A rich man, however, has so much that he stays awake worrying" (Eccl. 5:10–12).

"Invest your money in foreign trade, and one of these days you will make a profit. Put your investments in several places—many places even—because you never know what kind of bad luck you are going to have in this world" (Eccl. 11:1–2).

In the early days of the church the apostles "turned the world upside down" by living out Christian principles and preaching them to others (Acts 17:6). We get the same results today when we apply the principles of faith: it turns every area of our lives upside down—for our benefit. So I began applying biblical principles to the investment process. And guess what! It turned the investment pyramid upside down.

As a result, my financial life has become very uncomplicated, and this has affected every other area of my life. Since I am no longer so concerned with getting rich, I now have more time to read the Bible, more time to spend with my beautiful family, more time to serve on my church finance committee and work with the planned giving officer. And I can now sleep at night.

Yet my investment plan has never done better. I have discovered that making my money conservatively productive for God's family around the world is one of the surest ways of making it productive for my family at home. In addition, I get more than pure financial return from my investments. I get a good feeling inside about the work that the resources I call "my money" are doing for others, and I am relieved of daily anxiety about the future of my investments. This is security of the truest kind—when head and heart have the same goals in life.

Money is always productive. The question for the Christian is, "Who is it productive for?"

Money is always productive. The question for the Christian is, "Who is it productive for?" Depositing $100,000 in an interest-free checking account is very productive—for the bank. But the lost interest is unproductive for you or for God's work. The same amount invested in speculative penny stocks is very productive—for the people selling the stocks. But the losses will do little for you or God. An unplanned estate tied up in probate and ravaged by taxes is very productive— for attorneys and the U.S. Treasury. Bequests to your church or favorite charities are productive for the Lord's work.

Suppose proper financial planning could lift the average earnings on your money from 7% to 8% (in financial terms, that means you are increasing the return on your money by over 14%). You could use 10% of that interest for God's work and still have more for your family. That may not sound significant, but just think about what multiplication of that could do. Or think of the example cited by Cal Thomas, the nationally syndicated columnist, who has said that the welfare rolls of America would disappear if each church adopted just one family.

John Wesley said, "True religion [a personal relationship with Jesus Christ] will result in the people of a nation becoming more hard-working, honest, frugal, and thrifty, which results in the creation of wealth." These characteristics are 180 degrees away from the consumerism and low-productivity syndrome that has afflicted America in recent decades. I personally believe that our country would not have budget and trade deficits if we would return to a value system based on the Judeo-Christian ethic.

The Cornerstone Principle

Actually, you will get far too little from this book if you only increase the return on your money. What I want you to do is discover the practical, powerful, and ageless message that is the cornerstone principle of this book: "Seek first his kingdom and his righteousness, and all these things [that is, the essentials of life such as food and clothing] will be given to you as well" (Matt. 6:33). I want you to do more than prosper financially; I want you to prosper spiritually. I want you to learn how to avoid the greed, stress, and self-centeredness so prevalent in investing today. Only then will you gain a sense of security, a peace of mind, and a confidence in your future that is priceless. Only then will your neighbor prosper from your activities.

The plan is simple. Each of us must do his or her part to bring our lives, including our financial planning, into conformity with biblical principles. Deceptively simple, but so critically important to grasp.

Security and satisfaction are dependent on our state of mind, not on the state of our finances.

The author of Proverbs and Ecclesiastes said that the pursuit of wealth is like "chasing the wind." He could have been writing about our situation today. Recently the national accounting firm of Ernst & Young reported the results of a financial survey they had conducted. The respondents had an average income of $194,000 and assets of $750,000; yet the survey reported that 40% did not feel financially secure and *two-thirds felt guilty about being affluent.* I've personally worked with clients who are worth hundreds of millions of dollars and who still feel they need more. I can guarantee that wealth does not guarantee happiness.

Security and satisfaction are dependent on our state of mind, not on the state of our finances. If we expect wealth to provide these rewards, we are in for a lifetime of futility. No financial book ever written, no investment program ever devised, can make us truly "rich."

Objectives

I have no desire to develop some deep theological concept about "God's Master Financial Plan," for I am neither a theologian nor a trained Bible scholar. Aside from which, the focus of faith is more concerned with spiritual needs than with investment problems. However, if we are to realize that the principles of the Christian faith can address any modern concern, a basic theological understanding is critical. Therefore, I have simply looked, and continue to look, for those principles that might apply. What I have found during the past two years is probably best expressed in the five goals I have established for this book:

First, *I want to help you clearly understand the nature of money.* Money is neither good nor bad. It can be used with prudence and charity or with speculation and greed. The Christian ethic encourages prudent investment for the good of all, while the world today too often encourages speculation for the sole benefit of the speculator. For the Christian this produces internal conflict and destroys the peace we all seek. And it doesn't do our finances any good either.

Second, *I want to help you with the practical aspects of investing.* Most of the problems investors face can be attributed to one thing: self-centeredness. Banks, investment firms, the media, and many governmental entities care only about their own agendas. Investment counselors become thoughtlessly self-centered when they create fees for themselves but little financial benefit for their clients. And individual investors flirt with greed, always trying to earn just a little more return, regardless of how their investment dollars are employed. Two hundred years ago, Adam Smith, the father of modern economics, said that self-interest could be good for all of a society if it was enlightened by moral values. If not, self-interest could destroy a society. My desire is to help you integrate moral values and economic values into practical, modern financial planning.

Most of the problems investors face today can be attributed to one thing: self-centeredness.

Third, *I want to help you understand that as a Christian investor you are not just making a return on your money; you are making decisions that shape our society, whether you wish to or not.* By investing in bonds you can finance homes and education for low-income and moderate-income families, or you can finance the hostile takeovers of large corporations. Your certificates of deposit can finance inner-city housing for the poor and minorities, or they can bankroll massive credit card operations. You can invest long-term in ethically managed, environmentally sensitive companies and productive real estate, creating real wealth for our country, or you can simply gamble for other people's money. Jobs for those who want to work, homes for those who need them, and efficient production facilities for worthwhile businesses can make our world a better place in which to live.

If you apply Christian principles to your financial life, I can promise you the most prosperous risk-reward relationship possible. But take note: I cannot promise you the highest possible return each year. You can get that promise from advertisements and performance rankings in any financial publication around today—if you can live with the fact that each year the ads come from a different promotor, and that the highest performance rankings are often for yesterday's investments and those that took the highest risks. Current hot-streaks always turn cold eventually; eternal principles do not. The prudent road to financial security is not a crowded pathway, but it is a sure one.

Fourth, *I would like this book to serve as a desktop reference for clergy, planned giving officers, and laypeople interested in helping others with financial concerns.* We need to be aware that Christianity doesn't just provide answers for 10% of our money, any more than it only provides a way to live on Sunday morning. In the Word and through the Spirit, God has given us guidelines for living productively every day of the week, which includes the use of all our resources.

The notion that the church should concern itself with spirituality and leave the handling of money to the secular world is fairly prevalent today. But the Bible passages concerning money, property rights, fair financial treatment of the needy, materialism, and approaches to giving are not quaint items of purely historical interest, and I hope to prove this to you as I attempt to adapt these guiding principles to the individual needs of Christians in the modern world. It is possible to worship God in solitude, but if we are to truly serve God, we must be aware of how our daily activities affect our neighbors.

Savings and loan institutions, banks, investment firms, mutual funds, and even some evangelists spent considerable advertising dollars during the 1980s asking us for our money. They spent far less telling us what they planned to do with that money. Many of my associates in both the investment world and the religious community believe people like it that way. I don't buy that at all. I believe most people would like to know how to evaluate their financial decisions and perhaps prevent a repetition of the folly of this past decade. And Christians simply must.

In his classic work about Christian principles, *The Screwtape Letters*, C. S. Lewis records the imaginary correspondence between an experienced devil named Screwtape and his nephew Wormwood. Wormwood is a young devil doing his best to create mischief on earth but is rather naive in his approaches and understanding of human nature. In one particularly wonderful letter Screwtape sums up his experience over the centuries: "It is funny how mortals always picture us as putting things into their minds: in reality our best work is done by keeping things out."

I think Lewis is saying that we do not achieve peace through blissful ignorance, but by making the tough, thoughtful choices that reflect our faith. These choices will also prosper us in the financial area, and will certainly prosper our children and grandchildren.

In the early days of the church the apostles realized that they couldn't attend to the spiritual needs of the world around them if they had to attend to the pressing daily needs of the congregation. So they organized a group of lay helpers, led by Stephen, to deal with such concerns (Acts 6:1–6). Today our spiritual leaders use Scripture and theology to blueprint a marvelous world of peace, justice, and humanity. Yet this effort is of minimal value unless the plans are implemented by the people in the pews. When we (each of us) make our handling of money an integral part of our love for God, our neighbor, and ourselves, we begin prudently financing what we caringly preach.

If faith can accomplish great things with our tithes, think what amazing things could be done if we allowed

---

Goals for This Book

1. To help you understand that the nature of money is neither good nor bad.

2. To help you with the practical aspects of investing.

3. To help you understand that as a Christian investor you are not just making a return on your money; you are making decisions for our society, whether you want to or not.

4. To serve as a desktop reference for clergy, planned giving officers, and laypeople interested in helping others with financial concerns.

5. To help you inspire your own investment planner or banker, Christian or non-Christian.

---

our faith to inspire what we do with the rest of our money. It is one of my major goals to destroy forever the myth that only the money given to charity can provide benefits for humanity and glorify God. There is no reason that money should benefit only the owners of that money, and I hope to show you ways to use all of your assets to create a better world for you and your neighbor. A 10% tithe cannot correct a 90% abuse.

And fifth, *I would like you to share this book with your present investment planner or banker, whoever that might be.* When I say this, I am not suggesting that everyone should dash out and find a Christian financial counselor. While I do think that it is a good idea to seek a Christian investment planner or banker when possible, creating one could be even better. I would therefore suggest that readers take this book to their present investment counselors and ask them to read it. If they hesitate, tell them that 90% of all Americans identify in some way with the Christian faith (the fact that far fewer actually practice it can remain our little secret). Tell them that many people, yourself included, are not totally satisfied with the financial guidance they've received in the past, and that too few planners and bankers seem to know much about both a caring and a prudent approach to investing. If we are willing to do this, we just might shine some Light on a rather dimly lit Street.

2

The Christian Perspective

Discipline begets abundance, and abundance, unless we take the utmost care, destroys discipline; and discipline in the fall pulls down abundance.

A Medieval Monk

TO UNDERSTAND THE HEART and soul of democracy without studying the lives and works of Washington, Jefferson, and Lincoln would be impossible. To attempt to understand ethical economics without studying Abraham, Moses, and Jesus would be equally limiting. If we want a better understanding of where we're going, we always need to look carefully at where we've been.

Shortly after the record of Creation and the Flood at the beginning of the Old Testament we come to the story of Abraham.

Abraham's family was wealthy. They were nomads who lived in tents and measured their worth in children, land, and flocks and herds. If you follow Abraham and his descendants through succeeding generations, you'll notice that while silver and gold are mentioned, they seem of considerably less value than children, livestock, green pastures, flowing rivers, and the Promised Land of milk and honey.

Generations later, as the Israelites prepared to begin their exodus from slavery in Egypt, God told them to collect silver and gold from their Egyptian masters to take with them (Exod. 3:22; 12:35). (This does not refer to coined money, but to objects made of gold and silver, such as jewelry and household items.) God had promised Abraham that after Israel served for 400 years they would leave Egypt with great possessions, and this seemed to be one of the ways the Almighty provided for them (Gen. 15:14). It was not long, however, before the Israelites defiled God's gift by melting down some of this gold to mold a new god (Exod. 32).

Unfortunately this incident is not unique. As the Old Testament continues to unfold the spiritual history of humanity, we see God providing wealth, men and women abusing wealth, and people losing wealth because of disobedience to God.

The earliest provision I can find concerning the practice of tithing, giving 10% of one's income to God, is when Jacob offers to do it in Genesis 28:22. It is interesting that this follows immediately after the story of Jacob's ladder. In other words, one of humanity's earliest visualizations of getting to heaven was also one of the first real attempts to deal with wealth.

One of humanity's earliest visualizations of getting to heaven was also one of the first real attempts to deal with wealth.

From a purely economic viewpoint the most significant event in the Old Testament was the development of the Mosaic Law (sometimes called the Law of Moses or the Deuteronomic Law). The fine print of the Ten Commandments addressed fairness in business dealings; fairness to widows, orphans, and foreigners; financial guidelines for the priesthood, and related topics.

Two provisions that often surprise modern Christians are the laws that forbade charging interest to a neighbor who needed to borrow money and the laws that ordered all debts forgiven at the end of every seven years. While the Israelites were strongly warned not to withhold from anyone needing a loan, it is fair to say that these two stipulations effectively discouraged widespread debt. Giving rather than lending was the primary means of care for those in need.

A substantial portion of the Mosaic Law concerned real estate since it was the major source of wealth in that agricultural society. God's basic guideline is summarized in Leviticus 25:14–16: "So when you sell your land to your fellow Israelite or buy land from him, do not deal unfairly. The price is to be set according to the number of years the land can produce crops before the next Year of Restoration. If there are many years, the price shall be higher, but if there are only a few years, the price shall be lower, because what is being sold is the number of crops the land can produce."

The Year of Restoration (also known as the Year of Jubilee) occurred every fifty years, at which time the land was to be returned to its original owner. These laws discouraged speculation on the future value of the land, setting its price at its true worth—its usefulness. These rules kept real estate affordable and also allowed time for reflection about any transaction. The latter, in turn, encouraged fair dealings when buying and selling. In addition there were separate provisions to protect the interests of widows, priests, and the poor, along with special arrangements to protect those who had fallen into trouble with the law.

Moses' economic approach is summarized by a passage from his farewell speech to the Israelites. The great patriarch knew he was about to die and was leaving guidance for future generations, which certainly includes us:

> You will again obey the LORD and follow all his commands I am giving you today. Then the LORD your God will make you most prosperous in all the work of your hands and in the fruit of your womb, the young of your livestock and the crops of your land. The LORD will again delight in you and make you prosperous, just as he delighted in your fathers, if you obey the LORD your God and keep his commands and decrees that are written in this Book of the Law and turn to the LORD your God with all your heart and with all your soul.

> Now what I am commanding you today is not too
> difficult for you or beyond your reach. It is not up in
> heaven, so that you have to ask, "Who will ascend into
> heaven to get it and proclaim it to us so we may obey
> it?" Nor is it beyond the sea, so that you have to ask,
> "Who will cross the sea to get it and proclaim it to us so
> we may obey it?" No, the word is very near you; it is in
> your mouth and in your heart so you may obey it (Deut.
> 30:8–14 NIV).

I have grown to love this passage and find it particularly relevant today. Most of us have little problem
accepting the first part, which says that God delights
to prosper us—in fact we love to hear that. However, a
very large "if" follows this assurance: God delights to
prosper us IF we turn to God with all our hearts and
are obedient to the commandments. This is a bit more
difficult to embrace, but not impossible. We do not
have to search the heavens nor cross the seven seas to
find what God wants us to do. The Almighty implants
it in our hearts and minds. Then it is up to us to obey,
putting God's commands into practice in our daily
lives.

Judges, Kings, and Prophets

The later chapters of the Old Testament record
events that occurred during harsh times as tribes
struggled to become nations and nations struggled for
justice and prosperity. Politics, economies, and even
religion became more formalized and interdependent.
People began to accumulate wealth as we might know
it. Kings built vast palaces for themselves and a temple
for God, while the rich of the land valued larger and
larger holdings.

Prophets such as Amos and Jeremiah called attention to the fact that people didn't seem to need God
quite as much when they pursued and obtained wealth.

In the sad histories of the judges, kings, and prophets we see clearly how economic cycles can coincide with spiritual cycles. When people prosper, they do not feel they have to depend on God; when things get tough, however, they return to God. And since increasing prosperity seems to be the norm, it brings an increasing lack of spirituality.

The New Order

In the New Testament we enter a more "civilized" world. The influence of the powerful, sophisticated Roman government was widespread. People began congregating in cities and towns, taxes were levied, money was coined more widely, and wealth took on a fairly modern meaning. The Book of James, probably written by the brother of Jesus, discusses the practical aspects of daily life at that time, much like Proverbs did in the Old Testament. James takes a slightly different view of wealth however.

> Now listen, you rich people, weep and wail because of the misery that is coming upon you. Your wealth has rotted, and moths have eaten your clothes. Your gold and silver are corroded. Their corrosion will testify against you and eat your flesh like fire. You have hoarded wealth in the last days.
> Look! The wages you failed to pay the workmen who mowed your fields are crying out against you. The cries of the harvesters have reached the ears of the Lord Almighty. You have lived on earth in luxury and self-indulgence. You have fattened yourselves in the day of slaughter (James 5:1–5).

Clearly, the role of silver and gold had become solidly entrenched in the economy of the day and was creating problems. After all, Judas betrayed Jesus for silver, not for livestock!

41

The New Testament also speaks of the rich in less-than-glowing terms, advises about the desirability of laying up treasures in heaven rather than on earth, and reports on the chastisement of dishonest money changers. Money was creating problems that Jesus and the disciples had to address. In fact, there are about 300 verses on money and possessions in the Gospels alone. The Bible contains about 500 verses on prayer, 500 on faith, and over 2,000 on money and possessions. The primary message of all these verses is that you cannot serve both God and money. In the Old Testament people worshiped golden calves; in the New Testament they began to worship gold.

In the Old Testament people worshiped golden calves; in the New Testament they began to worship gold.

While the New Testament amply warns of these dangers, I don't believe that it says we cannot have money. James 5:2–3 says that it is the "corrosion" of our silver and gold that witnesses against us. In other words, it is hoarded money—money lying idle and not used productively for God's work—that seems to be the problem. It is the love of money, not money itself, that is the root of all evil (1 Tim. 6:10). And when Jesus spoke of how difficult it might be for the rich person to enter heaven (the camel and the eye of the needle story), he followed it up by saying that all things are possible with God (Matt. 9:23–26).

The New Testament does mention some wealthy people who were disciples of Jesus—such as Joseph of Arimathea, who gave his tomb for the Lord's burial; and Lydia, who opened her home to Paul and his coworkers. There is no question, however, that there are few wealthy disciples recorded. Some attribute this to the fact that the time span covered by the New Testament is shorter than that encompassed by the Old Testament, but I believe the shortage of wealthy faithful is not entirely due to a lack of time for them to show themselves.

Faithful followers like the widow who gave her last two coins to God's work are more common, and they will be remembered forever for their faith (Luke 21:2). Passages such as this have prompted some to maintain that saving for the future indicates that we don't have faith that God will care for us, an arguably valid point. Those rewarded with prosperity and the righteous poor create conflicting images of prudence and faith.

Faith Versus Prudence

A young minister who had come to take charge of his first pastorate was dismayed to find that next to the church stood an ugly vacant house surrounded by a yard overgrown with weeds. He walked past this eyesore for months. Then one day he noticed that someone had bought the house and was moving into it. Slowly changes began to take place. The new owner painted the house and repaired the roof, weeded and trimmed the grass, pruned the trees and shrubs. One morning the minister noticed the owner working in the front yard and stopped to chat. In the course of the conversation, the minister pointed to the smooth green lawn and bright flowerbeds and said, "Isn't it wonderful what God can do with a lawn and flowers." To which the owner replied gently, "That's true. But you should have seen this place when God had it on his own."

We view the subject of money much like the Victorians viewed the subject of sex . . . necessary, but not nice to talk about.

All the world's resources may belong to God, but we are expected to do our part to cultivate them, bringing forth their usefulness and beauty; and I have yet to find a place where Scripture says that money is excluded from these resources. God may not need our money, but God's work on earth does.

However, I hear few reminding us that money is good when properly employed in God's work. Or if they do, in the interest of maintaining spiritual priorities this message is conveyed so subtly that it makes little impact. Chopping wood for the winter does not prompt great theological debates about whether we should trust God to keep us from freezing to death. But when it comes to money, as someone has said, "We view the subject much like the Victorians viewed the subject of sex . . . necessary, but not nice to talk about." We actually seem to fear the subject. For example, I have not read a single book about faith and modern financial planning that discusses planned giving, which is a tremendous tool for supporting God's work and God's people. Yet the work needs our financial assistance, and this is one of the most rewarding financial investments we can make.

When we do this, God multiplies the return on our gifts, but not in the way many suppose. There is a theory abroad—in sermons, in books, and in television evangelism—that says it is smart for Christians to give because they will get two or three dollars back for each one donated. I couldn't agree less. I don't believe God has ever promised anything as direct as that. Our true "return" from giving comes from strengthened relationships with God, our neighbors, and ourselves. This is bound to prosper us as we go about our daily lives. Simply "giving to receive" will short-circuit the love that energizes the entire process.

We cannot buy our way into heaven. Several Scripture passages condemn the hypocrisy of a tithe not given from the heart, and the minor prophets were particularly concerned about those who gave their sacrifices for selfish reasons. The proper use of our money may allow us to approach heaven's door, but it is our faith that unlocks it. Suffice it to say that God clearly prefers our hearts to our money.

Balancing faith in God with personal responsibility is far too difficult for us to accomplish on our own, however. We must look to One far greater than ourselves for the answers to such complex questions.

Authoritative Answers

When we approach the words of Jesus for advice or answers about handling money, we get many different interpretations from many well-intentioned people. Understanding Jesus' words can be difficult at times, especially for those who look on the surface alone, for he often gave seemingly contradictory signals. Jesus immortalized the poverty-stricken widow who gave her last two coins to the temple, but he dined with wealthy tax collectors. He fed the hungry multitudes but defended the woman who anointed him with perfumes that cost enough to feed several hungry people. He urged his followers to use their resources for the needy but refused to divide wealth between brothers. He said that his followers should not concern themselves with food and clothing, but asked how they could be trusted with the true wealth of heaven if they couldn't handle worldly wealth. He clearly respected diligent work, as reflected in his hardy band of hard-working disciples, but he rebuked Martha for being too busy to sit at his feet and listen. He told the rich young man to sell all his possessions and give the proceeds to the poor, but told a parable about servants who were rewarded when they multiplied their master's money through astute business dealings.

The key to understanding Jesus' teachings about money is to remember that he frequently said one thing but meant something far deeper. While illustrating truth to his followers, he avoided conflict with those who might condemn him before his work was completed. These brilliant teaching devices sometimes cause difficulty for modern Christians who do not want to be bothered with subtle nuances; like Sergeant Joe Friday, they want "the facts, ma'am, nothing but the facts." Jesus understood how important money was in the world around him, and he understood its potential problems, but he was always more interested in the spiritual than in the monetary.

Probably the most troubling passages to deal with are the ones where he uses money to make points that don't necessarily relate to money itself, such as his instructions to the rich young man to sell his possessions, give the money to the poor, and become a follower (Mark 10:17–22; Luke 10:25, 27, 29). Many theologians I have read maintain that this passage is about self-righteousness, not some revolutionary economic theory. Jesus used the subject of money to gently chastise a young man who was of the opinion that the only two perfect human beings on the face of the earth had finally met. (He arrogantly told Jesus that he had kept *all* the laws since his youth!) Yet I can't help wondering whether Jesus was also telling us to take a second look at our money if we get as comfortable with our faith as the rich young man appeared to be.

Jesus wants us to place our faith in him, not in savings, investments, institutions, or governments.

Jesus related to people across the economic spectrum—from the poorest to the richest, from the most trustworthy to the most dishonest. He made it evident that entrance to heaven was not contingent on the condition of one's pocketbook but on the condition of one's heart. Rich and poor can find answers in his teachings, but we must remember that his first public statement included the words, "He has chosen me to bring good news to the poor," and his Sermon on the Mount remains a bedrock statement regarding the ideal relationship between the two.

The general tone of his collected teachings clearly indicates that while money can be a tool for doing his work, he wants it to be subordinate in our lives. We can have it and use it but never serve it. Jesus wants us to place our faith in him, not in savings, investments, institutions, or governments. He demonstrated a knowledge of the usefulness of wealth (in one parable he told a steward he should have at least had the wisdom to earn interest on his money) but clearly realized its limitations. Without question, he understood that his people would find the truest form of security in their faith, not in their money.

Early Applications

In Acts it is recorded that early Christians took Jesus' teachings very literally and actually sold their possessions and lived communally. It must have been a remarkable period of caring and sharing. But it is also important to understand that these early Christians expected Jesus to return at any moment. With that immediate expectation in view, the development of long-term prosperity seemed very unimportant.

Later passages of the New Testament, such as the writings of Paul, begin to reflect a more prudent, less day-to-day approach to economic well-being as believers began trying to build a more Christian world, rather than simply waiting for the end of the old one.

The most insightful analysis I have found of the attitudes toward money during this early period comes from a book entitled *The Holy Use of Money* by Father John C. Haughey, and I encourage you to explore it for yourself.

From his study of the gospel of Luke, Father Haughey has identified four basic approaches to money.

The first is outright greed and reflects pure self-centeredness.

The second is a trust in both God and money and reflects a split-consciousness that allows one to try to lay up treasure in both heaven and earth.

The third is an attempt to master money for one's own purposes and can be either good or bad, depending on the purpose and choice at the moment.

The fourth is to subordinate money to human and spiritual causes and is the one Father Haughey believes Jesus encouraged by placing money under the reign of God.

Luke was a physician, so it is not surprising that he focused primarily on Jesus' desire to heal the spiritual illnesses he observed among the people of his day. Before a cure could be prescribed, however, the sick had to realize they were sick. To do this, Jesus told parables explaining spiritual illness and health in practical terms people could understand. This naturally included the use of money. In his book, Father Haughey illuminates the financial side of the money parables.

Jesus saw the pursuit of non-spiritual things as futile and a source of anxiety. He pointed out the birds and flowers in all their freedom and splendor and asked if material things could provide more. Then he noted that our attempts to fulfill our own self-determined needs only produce an unhealthy numbness and blindness toward God and humanity.

For example, the parable of the rich man and Lazarus clearly demonstrates how riches can induce an uncaring attitude toward the poor. The parable of the Good Samaritan poignantly portrays how empty religion produces one of the most severe forms of blindness, evidenced by the "religiously wealthy" priest and Levite who passed uncaringly by the man in desperate need.

The first parable that relates to money is the parable of the steward who was fired for mishandling his master's wealth (Luke 16:1–8). After he was fired, the servant re-evaluated his relationships and forgave many of the debts his neighbors owed to the master who had just fired him. Surprisingly, his master praised him for doing this. Father Haughey writes:

49

> Those who have wealth within the community are being told: Your wealth is in the members of the community now rather than in your money. You must see yourselves, your money, and others with wholly new eyes, eyes that see the eternal significance of being in this relationship to one another in Christ. Your money and possessions now have a purpose. Make friends for yourselves by sharing your goods with others.

By using their earthly wealth wisely and well, rich Christians can find eternal wealth.

The second parable is about the wealthy man who gave several of his servants a portion of his money and told them to put it to work while he was away (Luke 19:12–23). One servant multiplied the money in his care ten times during his master's absence, and another multiplied his portion five times. But a third servant simply kept his master's money safe and intact as it was. When the master returned, he praised the first two for their faithfulness. But the third servant was rebuked, and his money was taken away and given to the servant who had increased his tenfold.

Father Haughey notes that Jesus is showing that although the wealth does not belong to the people controlling it, they are to use it creatively:

> The central issue of the parable is that a reflective, creative, and resourceful use of one's resources is the ever-present way those who are awaiting the fullness of the reign of God have of growing in Christ and pleasing God.

In other words, this is a serious attempt at what we call stewardship.

The third parable is about the Pharisee and the tax collector (Luke 18:10–14). Both men went to the temple to pray. The Pharisee openly fasted and tithed and thanked God that he was not like the tax collector.

Meanwhile the tax collector stood quietly on the sidelines, feeling unworthy of approaching God and asking for mercy. Jesus rebuked the Pharisee and justified the tax collector. Father Haughey writes:

> Religious acts such as thanksgiving and tithing in Jesus' perception often served only to delay self-knowledge and obscure the need for conversion in many. They substituted the ritualization of belief for belief. They did not see that their trust was in themselves and in their own abilities to perform acts of religion, not to mention in sufficient wealth to have the luxury and the leisure to be able even to consider tithing. . . . Unexamined religious rituals can conceal most of all to those practicing them the truth of the relationship one has to God.

Simply giving thanks and tithing leaves considerable room to mess things up with the rest of our money and time.

The fourth parable is about the rich man who had such a good harvest that he didn't have room in his barns to store it all (Luke 12:16–21). He decided to build larger barns, hoard all his wealth, and enjoy the good life for years to come. But God declared him a fool, demanded his soul that night, and asked who would enjoy his wealth then. Father Haughey writes:

> [Jesus] takes the major activity of those whose energy goes into mammon and holds it up to ridicule. This activity is accumulation. . . . On the face of it this seems a bit harsh [declaring the man a fool] since he didn't do anything morally wrong. Wasn't he, after all, just being a good steward of his bumper crop? . . . In this parable the fool's basic mistake is confusing his life with his possessions. . . . His relationships to others and to God do not enter into his decisions about his self-immersion.

The fool's basic mistake was blind accumulation.

Father Haughey also refers to the story of Zacchaeus, the wealthy tax collector whom Jesus called down out of a tree (Luke 19:2).

First of all, observes Haughey, Jesus made no mention of Zacchaeus's wealth. If anything, he availed himself of it by staying in the man's home that evening.

Second, Zacchaeus was seemingly one of the least likely persons of his day to enter heaven. He was a wealthy tax-collector and a social outcast. Yet he was set free of his past, his status, and his dependence on money by Jesus' simple act of acceptance and love.

Third, Zacchaeus demonstrated his new spiritual health by giving half of his money away and making restitution to anyone he had harmed.

Finally, Father Haughey mentions the story of the rich young man who wouldn't part with his wealth to follow Jesus. Along with the points about self-righteousness, Father Haughey also senses the references to monetary concerns in this passage. The young man "sought God but on his own terms."

> The following of Jesus is not to be juxtaposed, added to, or accommodated to what one owns. The following of Jesus is not to be undertaken in the minutes left over after one has attended to what one owns. Nor is the following of Jesus simply a figure of speech. Making it so can obscure a deep illness. For some Christians, Jesus follows them, he is one of their possessions. . . . Luke was inviting his readers to reflect on where their hearts were with respect to Jesus. . . . Their use of their possessions was to express their deepest loyalty and love.[1]

---

1 John C. Haughey, S.J., *The Holy Use of Money* (New York: Doubleday & Company, Inc., 1986). Used by permission.

The Last 2000 Years

The rest of the Bible—and history—continues this pattern of either acceptance or rejection of Jesus' challenge to human nature and the status quo. The choice has always been ours to make, but some of the Christian struggles with money over the last two thousands years are fascinating, illuminating, and insightful in helping us understand how we got from there to here.

For about fifteen centuries after Christ's ascension the Roman Catholic Church *was* Christianity—at least as most Americans perceive it. Under the guidance of the popes of Rome the faith spread across the continent, much like the Holy Roman Empire did. The church grew in size by sending priests out to evangelize the world. Since the world basically operated on a barter system in those days, these priests often had to farm so they could eat. Naturally they had to acquire land in order to do this, and they sometimes required a great deal of land since it was not unheard of for one-tenth of a town's population to be clergy. At one point, it has been estimated, the church controlled one-half of the land in France and Germany. It is important to note, however, that usually the local clergy barely made a living from these lands.

Monastic communities also sprang up, holding large tracts of land and a central church where the monks lived and worshiped. There they tended the soil, prayed, and meditated. This religious life was considered a much higher level of service than any other vocation.

During this period the church held conferences called "councils" where they worked out any problems that arose, including concerns about financial matters. It is interesting to note that in A.D. 325 the Council of Nicea continued to forbid the clergy to charge interest on money, while a council at Carthage in 348 and one in Aix in 789 objected to laymen charging interest.[2]

This religious system worked pretty well until about 1300. Then some serious problems developed in the church, and these grew for about another two hundred years until they were instrumental in ushering in the Reformation.[3]

Among the problems was the fact that many of the church's services had been reduced to money-gathering devices, and higher church officials began to live on a grander scale than princes and kings. Eventually the higher positions within the church were purchased by the wealthy for their financial benefits. It's been pointed out that the church's influence dominated largely because a king could make your life miserable, but a pope could make your eternity miserable! Many laypeople, and many local clergy as well, considered the popes and cardinals hoarders who drained them of silver and gold. This seems especially relevant for those who believe that the human race has hit an all-time low when some of today's evangelists use their positions for financial gain. As wise old Solomon often said, there is nothing new under the sun!

Around A.D. 1500 several economic and cultural developments began to clash with the abuses of the religious institutions. First, the shortages of the Middle Ages gave way to more efficient agricultural methods and more productive businesses. The average person began to understand what it meant to work for profit, not just for survival, and began to appreciate the

---

2 Philip Yancey, "Learning to Live with Money," *Christianity Today* (14 December 1984).

3 The following information and ideas are summarized from Harold J. Grimm, *The Reformation Era* (New York: The Macmillan Co., 1965).

benefits this afforded; consequently the common citizens began to question the heavy financial load the church imposed. Second, trade and commerce exploded, making the exchange of coined money a necessity. Coinage was controlled by governmental authorities, and the importance of the control of coinage was demonstrated by the French government around A.D. 1300 when it abruptly forbade the exportation of gold to Rome. This subsequently bankrupted the Vatican. Interestingly, the popes found a home in Avignon, France, from 1305 to 1378. Not too surprisingly, all popes were French during that period.[4]

The growing importance of the nation and the individual eventually encouraged and enabled some of the faithful to depart the church, led by Martin Luther and John Calvin and the other Reformers. Their ideas about spirituality resulted in the Protestant movement, which also had serious economic implications. In regard to the latter, their influence might best be illustrated by imagining Luther and Calvin picketing a monastery with signs saying, "Get a job!" And thus the "Protestant work ethic" was born.

It is important to understand that until this time work was considered a diversion from spirituality, and serious Christians only worked to the extent necessary to survive.

Both Calvin and Luther embraced the revolutionary concept that you might draw closer to the Almighty by

---

4 I would hasten to add that as a result of the Reformation, the Roman Catholic Church itself underwent a period of internal reform, and today that body is often on the cutting edge when it comes to the socially responsible use of money. Some might even say a rather lonely edge. As a helpful example, I recommend that you check in your public library for their bishop's 1986 pastoral letter on the American economy entitled "Economic Justice for All."

working for God here on earth. Whether they understood the economic consequences of what they were doing can be debated, but the results speak for themselves: A dedicated work force for the developing factories of Europe and a people who would toil to carve new nations out of wildernesses. Men and women could now find harmony with God in a factory, on a ship, or in the home as well as by serving the church and farming the land. This was a turning point in human history, economically and spiritually.

Other changes also occurred. People no longer produced only what they needed; they produced enough extra to sell in neighboring towns, countries, and continents. This trade increasingly necessitated coinage, banking systems, and other tools of industry. And as surplus money accumulated, it was available to be loaned.

Now a major question arose: Since people were not just borrowing to survive but borrowing to make more money, couldn't the lender ask for a portion of the profit (in other words, charge interest)?

Luther and Calvin said maybe, but on a very limited scale. They actually proposed rules about who could borrow, for what purpose, and at what rate of interest. Basically both allowed interest to be charged for productive, secured loans, *but not for consumption needs*, and both felt interest should be held to about 5%. If a brother or sister was in real need, the Christian community should meet that need through giving or interest-free loans and seldom by lending for interest. The general rule was that the borrower should keep the money until it could be paid back. (Alas, the borrower set the terms, not the lender.)

Both Luther and Calvin believed in "shared risk" for secured business loans. That is, I could loan you money to start a business or buy a farm. But if your business or farm failed, I couldn't reasonably expect to get back my principal and interest and thus add to your misfortune. This was seen as an application of the Golden Rule and essentially assured that lenders wouldn't get too aggressive in making loans.

Now that I've made my banking friends nervous, let me add that the spiritual community quickly gave up on this in the interest of economic convenience and expediency. In 1638, Claudius Salmasius legitimized the charging of interest with his work entitled "On Usury."

About this time, the action shifted to a new arena— from the Old World to the New. There the founders of democracy attempted to balance religious principles with economic endeavors. It is difficult to find a better assessment of this scene in early America than in the writings of Count Alexis de Tocqueville, the French historian who was sent on a special mission to America by the French government during the early 1800s and became intrigued with the idea that a people who viewed individual liberty as God-given could also aspire to be "one nation" under this God. He discovered that the American individualism and sense of community could coexist because they were rooted in strong religious faith. While democracy fed the desire for individual advancement, Christianity fed the desire for the advancement of others.

To understand this in practical terms, I often visualize Tocqueville riding over the eastern half of our country and observing frontiersmen engaged in such common activities as "barn raising." This was neighbor helping neighbor to establish security for the bounties of their work and thereby helping assure their future well-being. I have little doubt that it was experiences such as this that prompted Tocqueville to mince few words in proposing that those who attended to matters of the Spirit could also anticipate prosperity in this new nation.

We who own the corporate stock and real estate of America should also be aware that one of Tocqueville's greatest fears for America's future was the development of a "manufacturing aristocracy." He believed that the political shackles America had destroyed could be replaced with economic shackles even more binding to the spirit of the average person. As the world becomes more industrial and increasingly embraces private enterprise, his words are becoming more treasured than ever.

And how is America faring? Is it what Tocqueville envisioned? I have found few insights as illuminating as those of Dr. Peter Berger, a professor of religion and sociology at Boston University. His work and writings are particularly fascinating and timely because he studies the economic development of the East Asian countries as well as our own. In this regard Bill Moyer's book *A World of Ideas* shares some of Dr. Berger's thoughts on why Japan, Taiwan, and Singapore have become such worthy competitors in the world marketplace. Many observers feel that the sense of community in these cultures results primarily from their religious teachings, says Dr. Berger. "Their community-oriented culture has been what economists call a comparative advantage. . . . Their hard work and their ascetic, self-denying, group oriented ethos has helped them economically."

Meanwhile, he says, America's "cult of self-realization and the pursuit of individual happiness, carried to this crazy extreme, is not helping us economically. . . . What is making us less competitive is that common effort for the purpose of a collective goal is much less strong than it was in our own culture a half century ago."

Importantly, he adds, "I don't think one should be religious because it's socially useful. Even if it were not socially useful, I think one should worship God. And there are other things I believe as a Christian. It so happens that if I looked at the same phenomena as a social scientist, I would reach the same conclusion if I were atheistic or agnostic—that the decline of religion in certain populations has had some social consequences that are unfortunate. Conversely, religion in most of the world, certainly in Asia, is a very potent force."

I believe that "reaping what we sow" is a fundamental principle of Christianity and directly concerns our role in providing our daily bread. But I also believe that we can't turn sown seeds into reapable wheat on our own. We're in partnership with God and humanity for this daily bread, even in our modern scientific world.

Conclusions and Challenges

Moses revealed God's economic guidance to a people about to live off the land; Christ revealed it to a people about to serve others for a living; and the Reformers revealed it to a people about to engage in business for a living.

Today's challenge is to relate the same principles to a people who increasingly live off capital (money accumulated in pension plans, IRAs, and personal holdings). This wealth is often represented by paper securities and computer entries on a monthly statement from the bank. We go to church on Sunday, read passages about using our wealth for the benefit of God and neighbor, and feel conflict because we aren't always sure how to relate our principles to this "paper wealth."

Virtually every Christian businessperson I know has asked: "What does the Bible say about collecting delinquent debts owed me?" and "What are those guys on Wall Street up to?" But considering our five-thousand-year heritage, perhaps we should be asking much tougher, but more beneficial questions:

- Why do others owe me money in the first place?
- Do I loan money because someone is in need or because my business is?
- Do I extend credit just because all my competitors do?
- Do I sell goods and services without initial guarantee of payment just to ensure the order?
- Do I have any idea what my bank, mutual fund, broker, or pension fund is doing with *my* money?
- Is this another case of ignoring God's guidance and then asking what to do when problems result?

As a businessman I have found it very difficult to correlate these historical teachings of the faith with modern credit and investment practices. But I've also come to realize that the lending, borrowing, and investing of money can rapidly upset the interpersonal relationships that God values.

Over the centuries Christians have had to deal with many different forms of wealth, but the principles have always been the same. For thousands of years the most faithful of God's people have worried about the proper consumption and use of the Creator's resources, and for thousands of years God has faithfully provided the guidance to eliminate the worry. I believe God has done this because Infinite wisdom knows that guilt and worry provide poor motivation for stewardship. We need to get rid of both. Love—for God, our neighbor, and ourselves—is a considerably more pleasant and more productive motivation.

3

Basics of Planning

OUTSPOKEN DRAMATIST AND ICONOCLAST George Bernard Shaw complained, "All professions are conspiracies against the laity." While that seems a bit harsh, Shaw rightly pointed out the job security offered by specialized professions such as law, medicine, and accounting. I'm hesitant to promote the idea that there is some kind of conspiracy among such professionals, but it does seem that many enjoy promoting a mystique that holds the rest of us at arm's length, making their services even more essential.

The Bible says that counselors are valuable, but it also cautions that we ourselves are to be diligent regarding our own concerns (a qualifier not usually quoted by said counselors).

Nowhere is this more true than in the area of finance. Ultimately, YOU are responsible for your own financial affairs. You may need professional advice at some point, but you also need a basic understanding of what is involved to ensure that the relationship is of mutual benefit.

When it comes to the subject of finances, confusion and conflict of interest are two of the greatest problems. Confusion on the part of the person seeking advice, and conflict of interest on the part of the person giving advice.

If the world were a town of 1000 people, only 60 would be Americans; but the Americans would have incomes fifteen times greater than everyone else in town. Yet only 2 out of every 100 Americans retire financially secure, and 25 out of every 100 Americans over age 65 continue to work because they do not have enough money.

This concentration of wealth seems to be intensifying and will only be reversed when more of us understand the true nature of money and possessions.

What Is Financial Planning?

"Finance is the art of passing currency from hand to hand until it finally disappears" (Robert W. Sarnoff).

"A study of economics usually reveals that the best time to buy anything is last year" (Marty Allen).

"The entire essence of America is the hope to first make money—then make money with money—then make lots of money with lots of money" (Paul Erdman).

"Money is like manure. You have to spread it around or it smells" (J. Paul Getty).

"A bank is a place where they lend you an umbrella in fair weather and ask for it back again when it begins to rain" (Robert Frost).

As this brief sampling shows, when it comes to the world of finance, everyone has an opinion or a theory. And when it comes to the specific area of financial planning, the same holds true.

One of my clients maintains that "financial planning is the orderly transfer of client assets into fees and commissions!" a sentiment probably shared by many. The most serious—and complicated—definitions come from the professionals, of course, but to me financial planning is simply "spending less than you make for a long time and being smart and faithful with the rest." Defining is not the real problem, however. Making the planning process work for you is.

It's no secret that Americans don't save enough to become investors. We are the ultimate consumer society, believing that the purpose of money is to have things and to have them now.

We all do have certain needs, of course, and responsible consumption can offer great joy in life. But Americans have elevated "needing" to a fine art. We "need" everything. The professions of advertising and marketing are based on this fact.

To get a better handle on what true needs are, let's look at "Maslow's Hierarchy of Needs" theory. Maslow was a psychologist who identified several levels of human needs that have to be filled, in an ascending order.

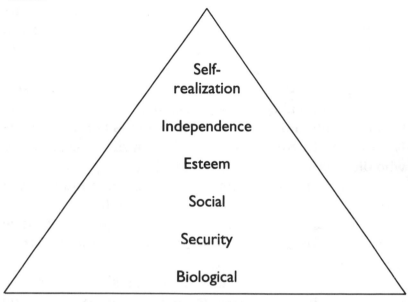

At the foundation are biological needs such as food and shelter. We brave the world each day to obtain these and establish the security of a job and a home. We join clubs or organizations to socialize with friends, where we might enjoy the esteem derived from heading a committee. You get the idea.

Merchandisers certainly have. They tie these basic needs to their products and tempt us with them, even though these tie-ins often have little or nothing to do with the product or service offered.

For example, bank commercials often show huge vault doors guarding our money (money the bank has already loaned to others), appealing to our need for security. Most beer commercials spend more time on the social aspects of drinking than they do on the product itself. Gucci, Polo, and BMW may all manufacture fine products, but their success relies on relating their shoes, clothing, and cars to our need for esteem, something that many investment firms also tie into. (If you think this is simply a "yuppie" problem, notice how our youth define themselves through their tennis shoes!) The rugged Marlboro Man urges us to express our independence by smoking his brand of cigarettes. (I've never figured that one out, but it's been incredibly successful!) And the consumer concept of self-realization (Maslow called it "self-actualization")—the feeling that one's life has been worthwhile—has been eloquently captured in the wonderfully apt bumper slogan: "He who dies with the most toys wins."

Critics of modern merchandising techniques often accuse them of promoting "style over substance." Style can add grace and beauty to life when it reflects true substance. But it can cheapen life and disappoint when it is a substitute for substance.

Now compare these Madison Avenue slogans with the wisdom of the Bible. Feeling secure has nothing to do with six-inch-steel doors, says the psalmist; true security is being able to walk through the valley of the shadow of death and fear no evil. Being social is loving and caring for one another. Esteem is found as we understand ourselves to be created in the image of God. And self-realization is hearing "well-done, good and faithful servant" as we leave all our toys behind and depart this world.

The financial point of all this is that God's plan for supplying our needs is given freely—there's nothing to buy. Society's answer is to buy THINGS, which must be purchased from savings or financed from future earnings. Isn't it obvious, then, that there's a better chance for you to reach true financial security—with its attendant esteem, independence, and self-realization—

through God's plan, which deals with internal substance, rather than through humanity's plan, which deals with external style?

If we are to achieve financial independence, we have to understand our true needs versus perceived or dictated needs. And true faith can be a tremendous, practical power in helping us decipher these needs and reach the financial security and dignity promised by God.

Materialism

There are far more important considerations than the financial when dealing with materialism, and we could write another entire book about the potential problems. But allow me to share just a few simple observations that relate to the focus of this book.

First, *the unqualified pursuit of large homes, prestigious cars, and other material elements of the American dream seriously hinders the relationships we have with God and with others, as well as our own personal and spiritual development.* It's all too easy for these objects to become all-consuming gods that demand our resources; cause us to cut corners when dealing with others; lead us into debt, placing enormous stress on our internal peace; and steal precious time from our prayer and Bible study, our families, and our church work.

Second, *our society makes it very easy to declare "who we are" through the clothes we wear and the cars we drive.* This can be a serious challenge to Christian humility and humanity. For example, do we buy Gucci because that company/designer produces a superior product or to make ourselves feel superior? One is fine; the other is a problem. If wearing Gucci tells us we're okay, will we no longer feel the need to be approved by

God (2 Tim. 2:15)? Can we buy Gucci products and still tithe, make charitable donations, and save for the future? Some of us can probably answer yes to all three—and some of us can't.

Third, *focusing on materialism often prevents us from seeing more serious problems.* For example, I've known Christians who believed that driving a prestige car somehow made them "better people," while I've known others who derived a sense of humility from driving a modest or economy car. I've known Christians who cut corners in business ethics in order to buy a prestige car, and I've known those who bought modest cars and then used the money "saved" in self-centered ways. One group derives comfort from "having the best," while the other takes comfort in the belief that "at least I'm not that bad."

All of these folks are deceiving themselves. After all, we can justify almost any activity we want by selectively comparing ourselves to others.

What seems basic to most Americans would seem luxurious to most of the world. For example, over 75% of the world's inhabitants do not own a car of any type. On the other hand, some goods labeled as luxury or prestigious can actually provide more real value and be less costly in the long run than many cheaper items that our "throw away" society produces—particularly if they are paid for fully after saving, tithes, and charitable giving, and are enjoyed in the proper spirit.

Lest we be tempted to rationalize too much, however, we should never forget that we must keep our enjoyment of luxuries in proper perspective while so many remain in need of the very essentials of life such as food and shelter—even in our own country.

The Financial Stages of Life

Life can be divided into five financial stages: protection, accumulation, conversion, preservation, and distribution.

The Protection Stage

This first stage begins when you leave school. At that point you have few assets other than youth and vitality, but they seem guaranteed for life. A word of warning: They're not! Therefore, it is of primary importance that you have enough money to support yourself in case of an emergency.

1. The first thing you need to do is put one to three months living expenses in a savings account or money market fund at your local bank.

2. Next, get an oil company credit card and begin to establish a good credit rating. Visa and American Express will vie for your business later if you handle this stage well. That means you pay the balance off monthly. While credit is dangerous when used to finance most things in life, it is an invaluable testimony to the world that you can handle money.

3. Assuming you are independent of your parents, you'll need protection in case you get sick or disabled for a lengthy period and can't work. If your company has disability insurance, buy enough to replace at least 75% of your income. Otherwise, call an independent insurance agent and buy a policy for this kind of protection. Be sure to notice how long the policy will cover a disability. Policies come in short-term and long-term versions.

4. If you are married and have children, you will need life insurance. Life insurance serves only one purpose: it provides for your family as you would have if you were there. To do this, you will need a death benefit of

approximately ten times your annual income. If your family gets this amount and invests it at 10%, they will have replaced your lost income. Get more if they can't earn 10% and if you need to provide college education for your children.

Life insurance comes in two basic forms: term and whole life. Term is inexpensive and has no savings feature built in. Whole life is term with some savings added. This savings essentially pays your life insurance in later years and may allow you to withdraw some money if you need it.

Term is the best deal IF you make yourself invest intelligently for the future. Agents usually try to convince you of the merits of whole life because they can make a better living selling it; however, they are right about its value if you have a problem saving and investing.

Financial Stages of Life

1. Protection

2. Accumulation

3. Conversion

4. Preservation

5. Distribution

Insurance companies are now developing insurance programs with more savings and less insurance. These policies offer decent interest rates and are currently granted some tax benefits that make them look fairly attractive. Read the chapter on insurance company investments before buying, and be aware of disability and death benefits offered by Social Security when making insurance plans.

The Accumulation Stage

Now that you are protected against most financial emergencies you can begin the accumulation stage, which is usually the longest and most complex period of our lives. Basically you will accumulate for three primary purposes: 1) a home, 2) education of children, and 3) retirement.

At best, Social Security provides only 1/3 of what you'll need to maintain your standard of living during retirement. At worst, I'm uncertain how Social Security will provide for future generations. To understand the situation, imagine you put $2,000 into an IRA each January. During the year you overcharge your Visa and have to "borrow" your IRA in December to pay your Visa bill. I think you can argue that you balanced your budget for the year; but I'm not sure you can also argue that you saved for your retirement. That's essentially what we're doing as a nation today with our Social Security system. Today's workers support today's retirees with their Social Security contributions and depend on tomorrow's workers to support them. (Really not all that bad from my perspective, as I don't mind caring for our elderly. But is Washington really turning generational care into a deceptive tax?)

Initial Protection Plan

1. Keep one to three months living expenses in a savings account or money market fund.

2. Get an oil company credit card and begin to establish credit by paying off balance monthly.

3. Purchase disability and/or life insurance according to your marital/family status.

71

A Home

Your first home is a bittersweet experience—the delight of ownership combined with the mortgage normally attached—which brings us to the subject of debt, the area of greatest disagreement among Christian financial writers. Most believe that debt is symptomatic of greed and impatience to finance what we have not saved for. Although I agree that this is often the case, I also believe that most people will never have a home if they don't take on the debt of a mortgage. Therefore, we need to weigh other factors into the equation.

Renting is the alternative to home ownership; but renting for much of your life carries many more negatives from a practical point of view and for this reason seems to me a very bad stewardship of resources. While you are paying out rent and trying to save the purchase amount, the price of the house you want will probably go up faster than your savings balance. Also, during that period you will lose favorable tax benefits and appreciation potential. Furthermore, the intangibles of home ownership, such as security and stability, simply cannot be evaluated in financial terms. With all these things considered, I view a mortgage as a proper use of debt.

I advise you to buy a *modest* home *after* you've saved 20% of the purchase price and are established in your career. Buy the least expensive home in the best neighborhood you can afford. Finance it with a fixed-rate mortgage so you don't risk losing it if interest rates rise.

Today many young people are financing their homes with variable rate mortgages. These often have low first-year interest rates that will almost certainly increase substantially in future years (even if the general level of interest rates remain level). This looks appealing but can cause financial strain in later years. Some people tell me they can't afford the fixed-rate loans, so they have to go variable. What they are really saying is that they can't afford the size of the mortgage, if they would only listen. In checking out your financial situation, the lending institution usually makes sure you can meet any increases, but they don't take into account your other obligations—for example, they don't ask whether you can continue to tithe and save for your future and still meet your mortgage payments. Variable rate mortgages have the potential to be very expensive in the long run and may be a form of speculation.

Many young people view a home as an investment. They commit to large mortgage payments because they think it is a form of forced savings. If you believe this, read chapter 9 on real estate investment.

Education and Retirement

Planning for education expenses and for retirement has produced more charts and computer printouts from financial planners than most people can absorb. These often do more harm than good because the goals they project are too intimidating. As a result many people won't even try to implement them. Over the years I have prepared many such plans myself, and normally I have found that while clients are impressed at first, they seldom do what the charts suggest.

I often recall some advice I got from a college professor in my business class. He frequently prepared business plans for the owners of small companies, and he told us that for a long time he didn't charge for this. But when he discovered that no one took these plans seriously, he began charging for them. Suddenly, when they had to pay for them, the owners began implementing the plans. His point was that it's human nature to only value that which requires a financial commitment. Eventually I decided that this could be applied to our personal lives as well. We only value that which costs us something.

We only value that which costs us something.

For years my parents told me that God could do more with 90% than I could do with 100%. Naturally as a logical, educated businessman I couldn't buy that. I had to learn the hard way that giving is a constant reminder of where I set my priorities. So I now have a business plan for my money based on the principles of faith. I use the plan because it costs me something in commitment, and my giving strengthens my commitment to the plan.

The first step in this plan is to put my money to work for God. By doing this I "invest" a percentage of my money in places that will benefit the church and those in need. This breaks the urge to accumulate for the sake of accumulating and replaces it with the urge to work for God and others. Giving should be the highest priority of a Christian and therefore should be the first priority for my money.

Step two in this plan is to give to myself. It's very important for *you* to be second in line for your money. You may not believe this, or you may even think you are already doing this, but think about it: Most of us can't wait to give our money to others who understand the true value of it. They ask us for it through ads on television, in newspapers, and in magazines. After they've gotten theirs, we get what's left and barely give God a thought. This reversal is the reason our financial and spiritual lives are so out of order.

In other words, *establish a giving plan with a matched-savings plan.* This puts you in partnership with God. Your interests are God's interests; they do not conflict. Then try giving God one dollar more a year than you give yourself as a reminder of your priorities. It will work.

Assume a young couple, about twenty-five-years old, can make $20,000 a year if they both work. They give $1,001 a year to God and $1,000 a year to themselves in an Individual Retirement Account (less than $40 per week). Even if their salary and giving never increase and if the earnings remain at an even 10%, which is historically justifiable as we'll see later, their savings will grow to $486,852 by the time they retire at age sixty-five! And while they may never directly witness most of the things accomplished by the money given to God's work, they will have contributed a great deal to that end.

Inflation can drastically hurt this $486,000 figure, of course, but most of us will be able to give and save more than 5% during our later years and we'll probably earn increasingly more as the years pass. Those two factors will offset much of the impact of inflation. The important point is that a systematic, prudent savings plan will adequately provide for your future.

One of the most important points I want to make in this book is the necessity to begin saving while you are young. Assume you save $1,000 per year during your twenties (admittedly difficult, but not impossible for those working rather than in school) and then stop (for a total investment period of ten years). You invest this money at 9% and make no more investments until you retire at sixty-five. At that rate your money will grow to about $310,000 by retirement. But assume you wait until you are thirty and start saving $1,000 each year until you're sixty-five. If you earn the same 9% on the money, you will accumulate about $215,000. By waiting those ten years you had to save $35,000 rather than $10,000, and you still ended up with almost $100,000 less! Incredible, but true.

A systematic, prudent savings plan will adequately provide for your future.

There are four important points in all this. First, in my example the young family gave 5% to God and 5% to themselves. Think what results they would have had if they had given 10% or more. Second, small amounts of money will grow to very large amounts over time. Most people rob themselves of the time factor by spending all their money on consumer items during their early years rather than saving. Third, our sample family saved only $40,000. The other $446,852 came from compounding interest. Fourth, earning an extra 2% makes an incredible difference over the years. There is no need to grab for the huge returns promised by get-rich-quick schemes. *These four points are very, very important. Think about them and review them often.*

I purposely chose the 5% figure, rather than 10%, for my matched-giving illustration because I am uncertain what a "biblical tithe" is. (Actually, most churches would be very happy if its younger members gave 5%!) Is it 10% before taxes? 10% after taxes? Does 10% apply for all income levels or is it simply a minimum guideline as it was in the time of Jesus? Can it mean 5% while we're young and have heavy obligations and lower incomes, but 15% when we're older and have

The Magic of Compounding Interest

My friends at Roxbury Capital Management in Los Angeles like to graphically demonstrate the power of compounding with the following example:

"Van Gogh's 'Irises,' painted in 1889, was purchased by Joan Whitney Payson in 1947 for approximately $80,000. On November 11, 1987, her son, John Whitney Payson, sold this painting for $53.9 million, the highest price ever paid for an artwork at auction."

Roxbury has computed the annual return of this phenomenal growth to be just 17.7%.

$80,000 Compounded

End of year:	@ 20.0%/year	@ 17.7%/year	@ 15.0%/year
5	$ 199,065	$ 180,706	$ 160,908
10	495,339	408,183	323,645
15	1,232,561	922,013	650,964
20	3,067,008	2,082,664	1,309,322
25	7,631,697	4,704,371	2,633,516
30	18,990,105	10,626,344	5,296,942
35	47,253,458	24,003,037	10,654,041
40	117,581,725	54,218,625	21,429,083

fewer obligations and higher incomes? Can I give 5% to church and 5% to my favorite charities? Is a 10% tithe even appropriate in our modern society where part of our taxes fund social programs that care for the needy?

Questions like this have troubled Christians for years. Interestingly enough, however, I've usually found *they are asked by those wanting to decrease their giving, not those interested in increasing it.* And church leaders seldom offer ready answers. In fact, many well-meaning leaders simply disagree about the subject. I personally feel totally unqualified to answer these questions, but my plan for matched savings and giving is built around partnership with God. If I slight God, I slight myself. If I prosper God, I prosper myself. This keeps me from asking too many questions that only confuse the issue.

I also know that my personal giving is a reliable indicator of the health of my relationship with God, and I want to do what I can to keep such legalistic considerations from making it less free, meaningful, joyful, and generous. If church leaders simply dictated some hard and fast rules about what size checks I should write, my giving would no longer be a voluntary commitment and personal effort. While their thoughts and guidance on the subject are appreciated and even helpful, I'm not really sure it's in anyone's best interest to make tithing anything but a very personal relationship and partnership between God and giver.

Consumer Debt

All your accumulations—whether homes, cars, or furniture—will either be paid for from past earnings or financed from future earnings, so debt becomes an important topic during this stage of life. As a rule—with the exception of a home mortgage—I discourage debt. Americans have become addicted to it. The recent years of high inflation taught us to be debtors rather than lenders; we could deduct interest expense from our tax bills, and government policies encouraged fixed interest rates at reasonable levels. All that has changed, but most Americans haven't seemed to notice.

Debt of any kind is expensive, but going into debt to finance cars, furniture, and other goods is so expensive

ACCUMULATION TABLE

Dollar amounts indicate accumulation at end of specific time periods of $1,000 invested each year at different compound rates of interest.

Example: $1,000 invested at 6% each year for 10 years would be worth $13,972 at the end of that time period. $1,500 invested at 6% each year for 10 years would be worth $20,958 (1.5 x 13,972). $2,000 invested at 8% each year for 15 years would be worth $58,648 (2 x 29,324).

Time Period

Rate of Interest	5 years	10 years	15 years	20 years	25 years	30 years	35 years	40 years
5	5,802	13,207	22,657	34,719	50,113	69,761	94,836	126,840
5½	5,889	13,584	23,641	36,786	53,966	76,419	105,765	144,119
6	5,975	13,972	24,673	38,993	58,156	83,802	118,121	164,048
6½	6,064	14,372	25,754	41,349	62,715	91,989	132,097	187,048
7	6,153	14,784	26,888	43,865	67,676	101,073	147,913	213,610
7½	6,244	15,208	28,077	46,553	73,076	111,154	165,820	244,301
8	6,336	15,645	29,324	49,423	78,954	122,346	186,102	279,781
8½	6,429	16,096	30,632	52,489	85,355	134,773	209,081	320,816
9	6,523	16,560	32,003	55,765	92,324	148,575	235,125	368,292
9½	6,619	17,039	33,442	59,264	99,914	163,908	264,649	423,239
10	6,716	17,531	34,950	63,002	108,182	180,943	298,127	466,852
11	6,913	18,561	38,190	71,265	126,999	220,913	379,164	645,827
12	7,115	19,655	41,753	80,699	149,334	270,293	483,463	859,142
13	7,323	20,814	45,672	91,470	175,850	331,315	617,749	1,145,486
14	7,536	22,045	49,980	103,768	207,333	406,737	790,673	1,529,909
15	7,754	23,349	54,717	117,810	244,712	499,957	1,013,346	2,045,954
20	8,930	31,150	86,442	224,026	566,377	1,418,258	3,538,009	8,812,629

From Joyce D. Sohl, *Managing Our Money* (p. 45).

that it can destroy wealth. Most consumer debt today is "floating rate" debt. This may look appealing now, but it will hurt you if interest rates go up. Actually, it is a form of speculation. You are speculating that interest rates will stay down, and we want to rid our lives of speculation.

A best-selling book of the early 1980s called *Nothing Down* encouraged people to borrow very heavily to invest in real estate. The premise was that you didn't have to have money of your own to get rich. Yet, almost without exception, clients I know who tried that strategy have been hurt. (The current best-seller, *Wealth Without Risk,* is how to get rich without risking anything. Ever notice how people are always eager for schemes that seem to require no commitment or investment on their part?)

Many people borrowed heavily to invest in the stock market before October 1987, and they also were hurt. I suggest that anyone who considers borrowing money for business purposes pray seriously before doing it. It may be God's will to borrow to start a business (or even to construct a church building), but the economics of debt are difficult. Remember, though it appears attractive now, the true nature of debt is revealed in hard times. And always evaluate whether you're borrowing from need, greed, or a desire to gratify your own ego.

Our attitudes about debt have even created a national and international problem as the United States buys more and more consumer items and borrows more and more money from Japan and other nations. Our leaders seem to have forgotten what was written almost four thousand years ago: "[If you do not obey the LORD your God] . . . foreigners who live in your land will gain more and more power, while you gradually lose yours. They will have money to lend to you, but you will have none to lend to them. In the end they will be your rulers" (Deut. 28:15, 43–44).

The true nature of debt is revealed in hard times.

In the early 1980s America was one of the largest creditor nations in the world (that is, we were lending to others). By the late 1980s we had become the largest debtor nation in the world (that means we are borrowing from others). Like many Americans, I would like to think we are prosperous because God has blessed us beyond any nation on earth. I'm afraid, however, that our seeming prosperity has been financed with a giant government credit card.

Furthermore, as a concerned Christian I have to question whether it is right to drain so much money from the other nations of the world. Is this a form of national self-centeredness?

I'm not an economist, but it seems to me that other countries need capital for their economies too. Many economists and government officials think it makes sense for other countries—even those that aren't so wealthy—to loan us money so we can buy cars, stereos, and other products. But is it right to buy "things" of limited life with debt that may accrue interest forever and risk our children's future well-being? Is this a form of generational self-centeredness?

Borrowing so heavily *for such non-productive purposes* does not seem to make common sense for our country, conform with Christian concern for other people, or conform to Christian thought over the centuries.

81

Financial Goals

Finally, I want to encourage you to establish four simple goals for the accumulation stage of your financial life:

- First, accumulate what you need while keeping faith with God and other people.
- Second, accumulate slowly, so that greed does not control your thinking and your life.
- Third, accumulate what you need without speculating about the future.
- Fourth, accumulate what you need in a way that will eliminate the stress that seems to come with most financial plans.

This is a simple plan. Resist the urge to complicate it. Be assured that countless debates, hours of analysis, and many mistakes by myself and hundreds of others underlie this simple message. (And enjoy the fact that I won't bore you with an account of them!)

A Plan for Spiritual/Material Harmony

1. Give a regular portion of your money to God's work and the needs of others.

2. Give to yourself on a regular basis—in other words, match your giving plan with a savings plan.

3. Use the remainder in a joyful but discerning manner for *your* highest interests.

The Conversion Stage

The conversion stage of life is relatively short and normally occurs at retirement. It involves changing your investments and business interests into assets that will pay you regularly. There are two basic ways to do this: humanity's way and what I'll call "God's way." This is one area where you can and probably should use both.

Suppose you've invested in real estate or stocks that have increased in value. Most people simply sell them, pay tax on the gain, and invest what's left in something that pays interest for the rest of their lives (such as CDs, bonds, or utility stocks). With "God's way" you allow the assets to be sold, do not pay taxes on the gain, and invest the FULL amount for income. This plan is discussed fully in chapter 11.

The Preservation Stage

The preservation stage continues from retirement to death. During this period most people simply want to maintain the purchasing power of the money they have already accumulated. Loss of purchasing power can result from 1) investment risk, where money is lost in a bad investment; 2) inflation risk, where your cost of living increases while your income doesn't; 3) tax risk, where the government leaves you too little; and 4) interest rate risk, where your income depends on the level of interest rates. We'll discuss each of these throughout the remainder of the book.

The Distribution Stage

Money that has been protected, accumulated, converted, and preserved must be distributed at death or earlier through gifting. This is discussed in depth in chapter 12.

Conclusions

Many financial plans are either impressively complicated or are designed to make you react by producing
anxiety over your future. A sales consultant, who may
remain anonymous, recently wrote in a financial trade
publication: "Unless you get the prospect emotionally
excited or disturbed with your opening words, you're in
trouble. Selling is a hurt and rescue business: if they
are not hurting, they won't do anything about it." Unfortunately, this approach occurs all too often in
American marketing.

Our less stressful approach begins and ends with
faithful, prudent saving NOW. America is caught up in
planning to save, planning to diet, planning to exercise—planning, planning, planning. I believe a small
amount of action today is worth a large amount of planning and delay. Planning can be frustrated by uncertain inflation numbers, uncertain taxes, uncertain
markets. In other words, most financial plans are only
as good as the planner's ability to predict the future. I'll
stick to the assurances we've been given that the future
will be fine if we are faithful to our principles.

Now that we've set the framework and tone for our
plan, we're ready to tackle the uncertain world of inflation, taxes, and investments.

The Big Picture

1. There is real power in saving small amounts of money over long periods of time.

2. The power of compounding can do incredible things if we give it time.

3. Beware of purchase plans and institutions that speak of "easy payment" schedules.

4. Reject the get-rich-quick crowd and emotional sales pitches.

5. Be faithful to God and self with your money and you will stay on track as you progress through life's financial stages.

4

The Inflation + Tax Equation

Few men have virtue to withstand the highest bidder

George Washington

IN HEAVEN OUR TREASURE will not be subject to the ravages of this world. Our earthly wealth, however, is subject to all the assaults this world offers. The New Testament speaks of enemies such as rust, moths, and thieves, encouraging us to put our money "in purses that will not wear out." At no time has that advice been more timely than it is today.

According to that great American sage Benjamin Franklin, "In this world nothing is certain but death and taxes." If *Poor Richard's Almanac* were in print today, its founder would surely add inflation to that equation. Because unless inflation and taxes are controlled and managed, they are a powerful combination of economic blows that can send you down for the count.

Inflation: Serious Problem or Casual Concern?

Recently I reviewed a study which maintained that inflation is not a problem for investors and should not concern us, reasoning that during inflationary periods, like the late 1970s and early 1980s, interest rates rise and we earn more money. This was based on a study of the past 35 years which showed that the interest rate paid on commercial paper (a short-term, unsecured loan to a corporation) averaged 1.55% higher than the inflation rate during that period. Inflation rose and fell, but the interest rates always went with it.

Whether they realize it or not, many investors already subscribe to this philosophy, for they use large portions of their money to roll short-term investments over and over. And because it appears that they're gaining each year, they continue doing this. Later I'll discuss why you should beware of first impressions and avoid doing what everyone else is doing with their money, but for now I would like to point out the negative results of inflation from both personal and investment viewpoints.

First of all, short-term investments cannot keep up with inflation and taxes. While the study referred to above mentions that taxes might have an impact, it doesn't really analyze how much of an impact.

Short-term investments cannot keep up with inflation and taxes.

If you deduct 28% for taxes from the interest you would have earned over that same 35-year period, you would have actually earned less than the inflation rate. In other words, you would have invested your money for 35 years and not gained anything in purchasing power. And if you consider that 28% was a low tax bracket during that period; that commercial paper is usually bought only through money market funds, whose management fees reduce your return; and that most people buy more conservative investments such as certificates of deposit, which pay less, you'll see that you would have suffered at least a 10% loss of purchasing power (and probably much more) by staying in short-term investments. It may make us comfortable to simply ignore inflation, but it's counterproductive.

What is even worse is placidly accepting the disease of inflation because we are blessed with money to invest and can more-or-less break even. When we do this, we ignore those people who are living on a fixed income, without money to invest, and who are seriously hurt by inflation. There is probably no single economic force that sweeps people under the poverty line as readily as inflation does. Being blessed with money in commercial paper, real estate, or other investments that seem to benefit from inflation should never blind us to the problems it causes for many of our brothers and sisters.

Also, this short-term focus has a domino effect for entire countries. Before inflation made six-month certificates popular during the 1980s, it was not unusual for my clients to buy eight-year certificates of

INFLATION. An increase in the volume of a nation's money and credit relative to available goods, resulting in a substantial and continuing rise in the general price level, or a loss of buying power (i.e., the ability of a nation to turn dollars into quarters).

deposit. When this was the case, bankers could feel comfortable using their deposits to make longer-term business loans or fixed-rate mortgage loans to those who needed them. But they lost that comfort factor when many clients started using six-month deposits and money market funds. Thus, everyone was forced to take a short-term view, and it became difficult to plan and use money for long-term benefits to society. As deposit bases became shorter and shorter, credit card lending, short-term consumer loans, and variable-rate mortgages became more important to our financial institutions.

From an investment viewpoint, inflation also encourages the problem that economists call "capital dislocation." That's an expensive way of saying that during inflationary times people move their money to gold coins, golf-course condos, art, and antiques. While Americans were doing that in the early 1980s, countries such as Japan, which have a better understanding of patience and time, were putting their money into factories and research for better products and services. The long-term implications for our children and theirs are obvious. Art and antiques may be nice to own, but they don't produce jobs and needed products we can sell to the world.

For these reasons and more, I believe that inflation is a very real problem and that Christian investors should do everything in their power to control it—especially now that the United States is the world's largest debtor nation. All we have to do is look at history and the serious problems other debtor nations have experienced with inflation in the past—the Latin American "Banana Republics" are notorious examples—to the point where a one-week deposit was considered a long-term "investment." Our nation cannot build long-term prosperity on short-term deposits as investment vehicles.

Our nation cannot build long-term prosperity on short-term deposits.

I like to think of inflation as the Almighty's reminder to Congress that only God can create gifts out of thin air. Essentially, Congress runs a "deficit" when it spends more than it taxes us for. Then the Treasury must either print money to make up the difference (which creates inflation) or borrow the money (which runs up our national debt). Either way, there is no "free lunch." President Carter had to print money; President Reagan had to borrow it. Presently, some of the experts doubt that President Bush can continue to borrow all we need (even from the Social Security system). Looking ahead, they foresee more printing, with its resulting inflation.

I agree with John Templeton that we'll probably never see a year when things cost less than they did the previous year. He's often called the Wizard of Wall Street because of his financial acumen, but he finds solutions to inflation in commonsense wisdom. Recently he was quoted as saying: "The currency of every nation is likely to be devalued. Those countries that will do best are those whose citizens are especially thrifty, diligent, and honest." He believes Americans will average about 7% inflation over the next decade. If he is correct, ten years from now prices will be twice as high . . . and you'll need twice as much money to maintain your purchasing power.

There are only two ways to keep even with inflation. 1) We can save extra large amounts of our income for the future, or 2) we can invest in areas that have historically benefited from inflation, such as real estate or stocks. The best way to handle it, however, is to encourage Congress not to give us all we ask for, or refuse to pay for it, and thereby put a stop to it.

Inflation . . .

1. is counter-productive

2. harms those on fixed incomes

3. creates a short-term mentality

4. encourages a low-priority use of money

5. is a symptom that we are kidding ourselves about "free lunches"

Taxes: Do They Manage You or Do You Manage Them?

The best thing we can say about taxes is that they do not discriminate— they hurt everyone. The worst we can say is that "sin taxes"— taxes on alcohol, tobacco, gambling, and state lotteries— hurt the poor more than anyone. "Tax shelters" are virtually gone, especially for conservative investors, so that only one strategy remains, and that is *qualified plans.* These are retirement plans to which investors can contribute without paying any taxes on the earnings until they are withdrawn at retirement. If any of this money is withdrawn before the age of 59 1/2, however, there are penalties, except in cases of death or disability.

Families making under $40,000 a year, or singles making under $25,000, should do an Individual Retirement Account. Self-employed persons and those who work for non-profit organizations should check into several other similar plans encouraged by the government. They are too varied to discuss here, but any bank, investment firm, or accounting firm can give you details.

QUALIFIED PLANS. Retirement plans, such as Individual Retirement Accounts (IRAs), which the government encourages by allowing certain qualified individuals to deduct yearly contributions from taxable income.

Also, you can move a qualified plan from one institution to another without paying any tax. For example, if your present IRA is not competitive, you may move it to almost any of the investments we'll discuss in this book without triggering income tax or the 10% penalty tax. Any institution that offers IRAs can give you details.

This is called a roll-over and is easy to do. Qualified plans can be very significant investments, so don't just do them for the tax deduction; make them productive.

Tax-deferral is a good tool, but not a perfect one. You must be especially careful if you anticipate moving into a higher tax bracket and staying there. Also, be careful about putting very large sums in deferred plans; this can become expensive later on. Very large plans can be sitting ducks for potential income taxes, estate taxes, and increases in tax brackets in the future. Seek tax counsel if your plans are becoming large. ("Large" varies with individual situations.)

> **PENALTIES.** When you withdraw money from tax deferred plans before 59 1/2 you must not only pay the tax on that amount, but a percentage of the amount (10%) as a penalty for early withdrawal, with limited exceptions.

Most of us do find deferral attractive however. Over 30 years, $10,000 earning 8% and taxed at the 28% bracket will accumulate to $53,659. The same amount invested in a tax-deferred plan at the same rate will accumulate to $100,627. Naturally you still have to pay taxes when you withdraw the money, but even if you pay 28% you would have almost $20,000 more. The advantage is even greater if your tax bracket drops before you withdraw the interest. (The chart on the next page may help you visualize this.)

The black line shows your salary, beginning at a low level during your early protection years. This climbs or grows during the accumulation period as you begin to earn more money. Then investments, illustrated by the gray line, add to your total income and usually increase your tax payments. It is during this period that tax management becomes crucial.

When you retire, your salary stops and you begin living on the interest from your investments. These payments remain at a rather fixed rate until the death of one spouse. (According to Social Security statistics, eleven out of twelve times the husband dies first.)

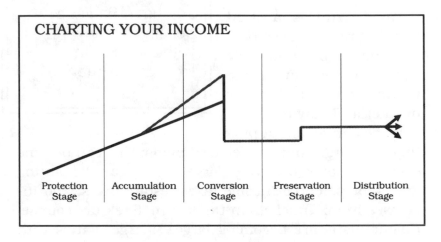

CHARTING YOUR INCOME

| Protection Stage | Accumulation Stage | Conversion Stage | Preservation Stage | Distribution Stage |

Two things happen here, as illustrated by the rise in the gray line during the preservation stage. 1) The widowed spouse invests the proceeds of an insurance policy, and 2) begins paying taxes as a single person. As you enter retirement, you need to plan for these contingencies by making projections that consider these two changes. A widow or widower should not be forced to deal with such painful concerns immediately after losing a loved one.

Also, widows are often sentimental about investments that were made by their husbands. For example, a widow may need dependable, tax-free income, but because she remembers how much her mate enjoyed playing the stock market, she'll keep his stocks. You should *never, ever* be sentimental about investments. The best way to avoid such problems is for a husband

---

Fighting Inflation and Taxes

1. Save extra large amounts of your income for the future.

2. Invest in areas that have historically benefited from inflation, such as real estate and stocks.

3. Invest in qualified (tax-deferred) plans.

4. Chart your income for tax management.

---

to teach his wife how to take a practical approach to money matters and what to do in case of his death (or vice versa if the wife handles the money). It's difficult to discuss our mortality, but being certain the one you love will be cared for after you're gone is one of the sincerest expressions of love.

Never, ever, be sentimental about investments.

One last point: I've seen people do horrible things with their money just to avoid paying taxes. Your primary concern when deciding what to do with your money should be to examine the investment merit; then, if tax advantages come along with the package, that's an extra dividend. But it should not be your first consideration. (We'll discuss such investments later in the book.)

We've been taught to give Caesar what is Caesar's (Matt. 22:21) and to honor and obey earthly government (Rom. 13). However, I'm sure Caesar did some foolish things with his tax dollars, just as our government does today. So there is no reason to give him more than he demands. After all, there is another Authority to whom we owe our first allegiance.

> Tax matters are subject to rapid and significant changes. Please verify the guidance provided here with tax counsel before use.

5

Principles of Investing

Good judgment comes from experience, and experience — well, that comes from poor judgment.

Simon Bolivar Buckner

THROUGHOUT JUDEO-CHRISTIAN HISTORY our ancestors survived economic cycle after economic cycle. From the earliest recorded time Israel saw years of peace, plenty, and prosperity give way to periods of famine, drought, and political turmoil. Better times always returned eventually (usually after a spiritual revival) but the severe testing and the lessons learned in the bad times bred a people of undaunted spirit and indomitable soul. The author of Ecclesiastes specifically cautioned investors about these inveterate cycles.

"Put your investments in several places—many places even," he cautioned, "because you never know what kind of bad luck you are going to have in this world" (Eccl. 11:2). Even today that's very sound advice.

Owning and Lending

Basically you have two choices when investing your money. You can OWN a business asset or you can LEND to a business, government, or individual. You own a business asset when you buy stock in Chevron, Chase Manhattan Bank, or the Kemper Insurance Company. You lend to a business when you buy one of Chase Manhattan's certificates of deposit, buy a Chevron corporation bond, or when you buy an annuity from Kemper Insurance Company (these will be explained later).

You own real estate when you buy rental property, but you lend to the real estate business when you hold a mortgage. You may also own your own business—normally the most productive area of ownership—or you may lend your money to a friend who owns a business.

Our economic system is designed to reward those who own businesses more than those who lend to them. People who use their money to assume ownership take more risks, and they will reap more reward over the long run if they run their businesses prudently.

Our economic system is designed to reward those who own businesses more than those who lend to them.

Many Christians are conservative by nature, however. They like to lend to businesses rather than own them, and they are willing to forego the possibility of larger returns for the probability of guaranteed returns. This type of person and investment certainly plays a vital role in our economy, and proper loans can meet some critical needs (many loans we make finance homes for young families and education for our youth). But I also believe that our economy could prosper in the long run if more of us did both. (Too few people seem to be using too large a portion of the available money today, and in ways many Christians might not agree with. Being an owner can mean being in control.) And I do not believe we need to abandon our conservative philosophies to do this.

Seven Investment Principles

America has become a nation of speculators; there's no question about it. We speculate on real estate, the stock market, bingo games, casino games, sports, and state lotteries. Financial advisers, gambling promoters—and even state governments—increasingly tell us that the road to riches is not working and saving, but hitting a "jackpot." Unfortunately many Christians neglect some very productive investment areas because they are afraid of speculation.

However, we don't have to become caught up in speculation—if we follow seven principles of investing. Principles that will keep our use of money prudent but productive.

Principle #1: *All, repeat all, investments involve risk.* You don't understand your investment if you don't understand its risk. And the higher the promised return, the greater the risk.

For example, in the early 1980s my clients who were retired told me that there was no risk in owning six-month certificates of deposit at 16% (thirty-year treasury bonds paid 15% at the time). They couldn't answer me when I asked them why this was an exception to "the higher the return, the higher the risk" principle. Now they know. They understand that the certificates of deposit paid more because they contained the risk of a 50% drop in income over the next few years as short-term rates dropped to under 8%, whereas the money invested in treasury bonds would have been locked in at 15% for years to come. Because they didn't have as much "interest rate risk," the treasury bonds promised less; but in the long run they would have delivered more. Notice that both are government guaranteed, which takes care of the "credit risk"— usually the only risk most people consider. But the other forms of risk are always present too.

Most conservative investors simply read ads and newsletters or call their local bank looking for the certificate of deposit or bond promising the highest interest rate. Although they don't realize it, they are really chasing the investment with the highest risk and employing the most disappointing investment strategy. Advertising, media listings, banks, and brokers have successfully trained modern Americans to seek the greatest promises. Far, far too few of these mention little or anything about all the risks involved.

Principle #2: *If it looks too good to be true, it is.* I believe the largest single obstacle to investing success today is that there are too many ways to make an average investment look extremely attractive. Clever promoters are always coming up with new ways, and we'll discuss some of them throughout this book. The best way to avoid them is to heed the old adage: "If it looks too good to be true, it is."

We consider it astute to shop the ads and institutions for the highest returns. But too much of this can lead us into hands that wield creative pencils and operate creative calculators.

It is very important to understand that the best ACTUAL returns usually don't come from the top of the lists offering the highest PROMISED returns. Historically, the best investments—stocks and real estate—haven't *promised* any returns at all!

Principle #3: *Be skeptical but not cynical.* Skepticism is healthy; cynicism isn't. Many potential investors are simply hiding in the foxholes as financial bombshells seem to explode around them. They don't trust anyone, including themselves.

My message is simple: The average investor is not really in a battle zone.

We may be led to believe this because the press has suddenly discovered that greed and corruption exist in the worlds of insider trading, junk bonds, penny stocks, and the commodity pits. Imagine that! But those battles are far removed from the domain of most conservative investors. Speculators can only kill you if you engage them on their short-term battlefield. If you arm yourself with a simple skepticism and stick to the productive, conservative areas, in the long run you'll be safe.

Principle #4: *What goes up will assuredly come down (at least for a while).* Very successful investors, like John Templeton, combine a faith in the future with a healthy respect for and an acceptance of the downs along the way. The world has always seen good times and bad times, and will continue to do so. However, throughout history the world has become steadily more productive.

Peter Lynch, who manages the very productive Fidelity Magellan Fund, doesn't spend any more time than John Templeton does trying to predict the short-term future of the stock market. Recently he was on the television show "Wall Street Week" and was asked how he would respond to all those predicting a market decline (he stays 100% in the market—meaning he doesn't switch from stocks to cash every time an economic indicator changes). He replied, "I tell them my fund will go down." He then went on to say that that was fine because it would give him an opportunity to buy stocks at prices he could tell his grandchildren about. Lynch understands—as very, very few people in America do—that a drop in the market is a buying opportunity, not a reason to panic.

Many analysts and members of the press spend a lot of time trying to predict the future. Their time might be better spent evaluating why people like Peter Lynch and John Templeton continue to make more money year after year.

The Christian faith cautions us about presuming upon the future. "Since no man knows the future, who can tell him what is to come?" warns Solomon (Eccl.8:7 NIV). That's good advice in the modern economic world as well. After forty years of dealing with the top brokers in the world, John Templeton still says he never asks what the market is going to do, since he knows *no one* can tell him that! And it's a lot less stressful than worrying about whether your predictions will come true.

Principle #5: *Fear and greed may drive Wall Street, but they shouldn't motivate Christians.* The oldest saying on Wall Street is that people invest the way they do either out of fear or out of greed. Those who fear losing money buy certificates of deposit and treasury bonds. Those who fear the effects of inflation invest in real estate. And far too many, out of greed, pursue their fortunes in strange ways.

Scripture teaches that we are to free ourselves from fear of the future and from greediness. We should be productive and prudent with money. Our investing will benefit greatly by remaining confident yet conservative.

Seven Investment Principles

1. The higher the promised return, the greater the risk.

2. If it looks too good to be true, it is.

3. Be skeptical but not cynical.

4. What goes up must come down, for a while.

5. Be confident and conservative, not fearful and greedy.

6. If everyone is doing it, it's wrong.

7. Those who prosper others will prosper themselves.

Principle #6: *If everyone is doing it, it's wrong.* The easiest thing to do with money is what everyone else is doing. The hardest thing to learn about investing is that following the crowd never works.

Remember when everyone knew inflation couldn't decline? And interest rates couldn't come down? And there was no more oil in the world? And you couldn't lose money in real estate? And the world was crumbling in October 1987? You get the idea.

Christians have always been called to be different from the rest of the world. Your faith will help you practice this principle, and your investing will benefit.

Principle #7: *Keeping faith with others is good business.* "Ethical investing," or "socially responsible investing," is based on the simple premise that investments that treat others and our environment properly will prosper everyone. I believe this MUST BE a cornerstone principle for any Christian who handles money.

Deloitte and Touche, the national accounting firm, recently published a study entitled "Ethics in American Business: A Special Report." The conclusions reached support what God has been trying to teach us for centuries.

Studies indicate that successful companies over the long term tend to be ethical companies. For example, the Ethics Resource Center in Washington examined 21 companies with a written code of principles stating that serving the public was central to their being. The Center found that if you had invested $30,000 in a composite of the Dow Jones thirty years ago, it would be worth $134,000 today. If you had invested the same $30,000 in those companies in the survey, your $30,000 would be worth $1,021,861 today—almost nine times as much!

In another study, Mark Pastin, director of the Center for Ethics at Arizona State University, found that a list of U.S. corporations that have paid dividends for 100

107

years or more tends to coincide with those companies that make ethics a high priority.[1]

A study by Johnson & Johnson indicates that 30 companies that were considered to have above average ethical standards significantly outperformed the stock market average. While the Dow Jones Industrial Average has risen fivefold in the last 30 years, the stock value of the 30 companies in the survey experienced a 23-fold increase.[2]

In other words, investing in companies with written codes of ethical guidance was nine times as productive as investing in the average company. Investing in companies that simply practiced above-average ethical behavior was over four times as productive! And in both instances income tended to be more predictable.

The oldest mutual fund associated with the ethical investment concept is called the Pioneer Fund. This fund avoids alcohol, tobacco, and gambling stocks as a matter of policy and searches for real value, not stocks that might just be popular at the moment. Also it avoids trading and holds stocks for the long term. I recently called them and asked for a computer printout of the results had an investor been able to invest $1,000 a year into an IRA (IRAs were not around in 1928, of course). The total investment for 61 years would be $61,000, but the account would have grown to over $20,000,000 by 1989. And the fund has never missed paying a dividend check, even during the Depression of the 1930s. Nor is this an isolated performance. The American Mutual Fund, the Washington Mutual Investors Fund, and the Templeton Funds

---

1 Cited by Kenneth H. Blanchard for the Deloitte and Touche publication.

2 Reprinted from a *New York Times* article by John S. R. Shad in the Deloitte and Touche study.

employ similar screening philosophies and have performed as admirably for decades.

This isn't to necessarily recommend these particular funds, but to make several important points:

First, you don't have to copy the aggressive trading strategies around today in order to be successful.

Second, you don't have to speculate about whether to put money into a fund or draw it out from year to year; just keep investing on a regular basis.

Third, you don't need to speculate to accumulate all you need. Pioneer has averaged 13% a year since its inception. Many speculative ventures today promise huge returns but carry huge risk. However, assuming prudent risk to achieve an extra 2% or 3% can be very productive.

Fourth, it is possible to give to God's work and still care for yourself.

And fifth, it dramatically demonstrates the merit of maintaining some ethical standards in your daily efforts. Today it requires little faith to invest in the

---

Ethical Results

1. You do not have to be an aggressive trader to be a successful investor.

2. You do not need to speculate to accumulate all you need.

3. You can apply your biblical/ethical standards to your investment program.

4. Having principles can increase your principal!

Pioneer Fund since it has an established track record. But those who invested with Pioneer over the years and stayed with them because they demonstrated some ethical concern have been amply rewarded. A valuable lesson for the financial marketplace could be hidden in this.

In 1988 two of the top five performing mutual funds in the country were ethical funds. (I've listed a few of the better known funds in the resource section at the end of the book.) As a result, several articles have been written about this "new" concept. Also, there is an excellent and very detailed book on the entire area of ethical investing entitled *Ethical Investing*, by Amy L. Domini and Peter D. Kinder. These authors point out that those who practice ethical investing represent a variety of interpretations of ethics as well as different screening techniques. Some organizations, such as the Calvert Group of mutual funds, specifically identify themselves with the area of ethical investing, while others, such as John Templeton, American Fund, Washington Mutual, and Pioneer, simply practice many of the principles.

Ethics and Economics

During the past couple years I have come to realize that most investments carry some ethical considerations. I have no idea why I had to go searching to discover that, but I did— probably because nobody really talks about it. Maybe it's because our society is too involved in taking care of number one; maybe it's lack of interest on the part of the financial press; maybe it's more convenient for investment firms and banks not to think much about ethics; maybe it's a lack of leadership from government in the area of ethics; or maybe it's the reluctance of business professors and clergy to approach the subject. Whatever lies behind this silence—actually, it's a combination of all of the above—there is no question that I had not deeply thought about ethical considerations as I simply looked to make a dollar.

What I didn't fully understand was that ethical considerations are as valid as economic considerations in making that dollar. So I spent hours futilely trying to predict the future of the economy and the markets when I should have been looking for investments that would provide solid, clean economic benefit to humanity.

You don't really need to be an economist or an investment expert to understand which perspective will be most successful in the long run. Many Christians starting a small business would never even consider investing in a casino, owning a liquor distributorship, becoming a weapons manufacturer, using near slave labor, or operating a lending business charging usury rates. Yet many of these same individuals pay little attention to the ultimate destination of their investments through stocks, bonds, and bank deposits.

Modern investment procedures distance us from how our money is affecting our neighbors. They are simply computer entries or a piece of paper. In some ways it's what happens when I give to my church. Too often I hurriedly write a check before I dash out the door on Sunday morning, not caring nor really thinking about how the money will be used.

At times I envy the Israelites of the Old Testament. How close to God they must have felt as they searched for the perfect lamb or grain, carried it to the temple, and watched it being offered and sacrificed. While I believe we can still give sacrificially from our resources in a proper spirit—perhaps even more so, when we contemplate the sacrificial offering the Lord has given for us— I also believe that the convenient modern methods of giving actually require a higher level of consciousness on our part. The same can be said about how our computer entries and paper investments reflect our principles.

Some church leaders have been actively trying to apply the Christian ethic to the economic community for years, but most church members are totally unaware of their efforts. For example, the Interfaith Center on Corporate Responsibility (ICCR) is a nationwide coalition of religious investors who "utilize church investments and other resources to change unjust or harmful corporate policies and practices, challenging the powerful role giant multinational corporations play in the use and misuse of the Earth's human and natural resources." Recently the ICCR published this in a brochure about the organization:

> In 1971, the Episcopal Church boldly made business history when it filed the first church-sponsored shareholder resolution calling on General Motors to withdraw from South Africa. Eighteen years later the corporate responsibility movement had grown to include activist churches and public and private pension funds with $400 billion in total invested portfolio worth and the ability to make a tangible difference in corporate behavior. The churches together with conscientious people from across the U.S. convinced over 160 U.S. corporations to sell their South African assets and U.S. banks to stop loans to racist South Africa. Churches persuaded numerous corporations to publish EEO reports, withdraw harmful or ineffective drugs from the market, change labor relations practices in Guatemala and modify dangerous baby formula marketing practices in the Third World to name but a few accomplishments.

Other denominations and groups try to use their bank deposits, bonds, and "alternative investments" for positive social good. Many of our denominational pension and endowment funds screen their investments and use funds to support the poor and minorities. Whether you agree with all of these efforts or not, they have proven that Christians can make a difference in this world by where and how they invest their money.

Modern investment procedures distance us from how our money is affecting our neighbors.

Throughout the church's gloriously turbulent history Christians have believed in the principles of fairness, thrift, prudence, and productive work. Those principles also built America. And they still offer some financial answers today.

It is only logical that our investments will be of benefit to ourselves and the world if we are not financing activities that 1) prompt large liability suits, 2) cause discrimination suits, 3) entice Environmental Protection Agency fines, 4) are subject to voter cutbacks, such as military contracts, 5) suffer from political turmoil, such as South Africa, 6) encourage others to become indebted to the point where they can't repay their loans, and 7) employ our money without producing any goods or services of value to our neighbor. In other words, we eliminate a lot of risk by investing ethically, and risk is one-half of the "risk-reward" equation that must be controlled.

Most investment professionals understand that avoiding the "investment risk" of such things as options, commodities, and junk bonds usually helps long-term investment performance. But couldn't avoiding "ethical risk" accomplish the same thing? Daily we are confronted with evidence that our society is too concerned about short-term profits and too unconcerned about the long-term welfare of others. Newspapers headline multimillion-dollar "churning" cases where investment counselors use client funds to produce commissions and little else; huge product liability cases among manufacturers; banking institutions becoming insolvent because of questionable lending practices, enormous bonuses to upper management, and too much interest to depositors; and enormous amounts paid out of corporate earnings to clean up environmental hazards. Forgetting the welfare of the rest of our planet becomes a very expensive habit for investors.

Or, if you want to be pragmatic about it, how many businesses could afford the sizable advertising budgets that would be needed to replace clients who left simply because their needs were not a top priority? While *faith demands* ethical behavior, haven't our studies convinced us that "good ethics is good business"?

Investment based on an ethical standard will be more resistant to economic downturns because it supports those concerns that fill a true

Avoid financing activities that . . .

1. prompt large liability suits

2. cause discrimination suits

3. entice EPA fines

4. are subject to voter cutbacks

5. suffer from political turmoil

6. encourage indebtedness

7. speculate rather than produce

need and maintain customer loyalty. At the risk of proof-texting, look again at Proverbs 15:6: "Righteous men keep their wealth, but wicked men lose theirs when hard times come." The author of Proverbs knew that any economic philosophy can look good during good times.

Forgetting the welfare of the rest of our planet becomes a very expensive habit for investors.

But most investors who financed the egotistical takeovers of large companies by buying junk bonds probably ended up envying Ginnie Mae buyers who, by helping others finance their homes, still received a sound and solid investment return. And those traders who zigged when they should have zagged ultimately envy the long-term investors who maintain their perspective and their return.

The sage of Proverbs seemed to understand what any experienced investment counselor can tell you about the laws of mathematics: they favor the investor who steadily produces modest gains each year over the investor who wins big one year but loses big the next. Ethical standards can help us achieve this mathematical advantage.

Specific Recommendations

For most people I recommend five investment areas that historically have performed well and that provide economic benefit to the world. They in no way represent "God's List of Approved Investments," but are merely an attempt to guide money into productive areas and to help the investor avoid greed, stress, speculation, and excessive debt. These five areas are short-term savings, insurance company contracts, bonds, stocks, and real estate.

Each of these areas has good points and bad. Unfortunately Americans continue to look for the perfect investment opportunity—which doesn't exist. Instead, we should look at ethical considerations and common-sense, practical considerations, both of which are often ignored in favor of the promise of a little higher return.

I grew up on a farm in Kentucky where we spent Monday to Saturday growing tobacco and spent Sunday discussing social problems such as the dangers of alcohol. In my current denomination we are allowed more latitude toward alcohol from Monday to Saturday but often have discussions on Sunday about the effects of tobacco. Because of this background and personal experience, I will draw as few lines as possible for you. In fact, I worry less about having good answers for today's investors and more about having good questions for them. What I want to do above all is MAKE YOU THINK about how you handle your money. If I can just get you to do that, I will be very happy. Then you can provide your own answers.

Don't expect to change the way you handle your money overnight. Many applications of Christianity are not easy to live with at first—I know that from personal experience. Just give it a chance. Four thousand years have proven how dependable these concepts are.

Part 2

Building Your Financial House

FOR HIS EIGHTH BIRTHDAY, Boomer's parents gave him a marble-making machine. That night Boomer made his first marble, and the next day he took it with him to his third-grade class at Central Elementary School. He showed the marble to his best friend, Justin.

"I can make you some of these for 10 cents each," Boomer said, "and then we can play."

"All right!" said Justin.

Boomer made Justin the marbles, and the next day the two boys played the game at recess.

Corey, another third grader, was playing tag with all the other kids, but he noticed the game of marbles. It looked like fun. That afternoon he asked Boomer to make him some marbles so he could play too.

Before long, most of the kids in the third grade wanted marbles, and they offered Boomer 25 cents apiece to assure getting them quickly. Boomer was so busy making marbles that he didn't have time to play, so Justin agreed to sell them for him for a 5-cent commission. Business was good and the commissions were steady.

The fourth graders at CES rarely noticed the third graders, but the marble games looked like so much fun that several of the fourth graders asked Justin to get them some marbles.

"We'll give you 50 cents each if you can get them for us," they said.

Before long the editor of the school newspaper picked up on the trend and printed a short paragraph on the sports page about the fun of playing marbles.

Now Boomer couldn't make the marbles fast enough. The shortage pushed the price of marbles to 75 cents each, and Justin's commissions got bigger and better.

Kyle, a sharp fifth grader, noticed the profit in the marble-making business. He got his parents to buy him a marble-making machine, and he began selling marbles to the sixth, seventh, and eighth graders.

The school newspaper ran a headline story, "MARBLES NOW SELLING AT $1.00," and announced that from now on there would be a regular column on marbles in the paper. They interviewed Justin about the "Make Money in Marbles" book he was writing and also spoke with Corey, who declared that he'd made enough cookie money for the entire year.

Everyone at Central Elementary wanted marbles. Kids who had never owned a marble in their lives and had no desire to play marbles wanted them so they could make money too. Justin, who was selling a lot of marbles and collecting a lot of commissions, began training other marble brokers. He gave seminars at recess on "The Fun and Profit of Marbles."

By now, Boomer and Justin had spending money to spare, and Boomer decided the marble business was getting old. Kids were still buying marbles, but the price was stuck at $1.00 each since so many kids were making them and selling them. So Boomer had Justin sell off the remaining marbles. They had to sell some for 75 cents because virtually everyone at Central had all the marbles they wanted. Kyle, who had also made plenty of money, noticed and sold out too.

The kids who had bought marbles early for 25 cents lost interest in the game and decided to take advantage of the sell-out, unloading their marbles at 75 cents. Other serious players noticed the price decline and salvaged what they could. Some had to sell for 50 cents.

The marble column in the school paper, read at Sunday brunch by the less serious students of the game, reported, "MARBLE PRICES DROPPING." Several marble experts who were interviewed for the article predicted that the price of marbles would soon reverse and continue upward. But some players decided they had better salvage at least 25 cents while they could. Fewer and fewer marble players were evident at recess. Then came the front-page headline: "DISASTER HITS MARBLE BUSINESS." Kids who had never really played decided they'd better get out fast, but no one was interested in buying. The marble market was dead!

Boomer and Justin, who still loved the game, offered to buy up the remaining marbles at 15 cents apiece. They figured the marbles were worth that just to play with at recess. The sellers accepted the offer since Boomer and Justin were the only kids around with any investment money left.

"The Rise and Fall of the Marble Market at Central Elementary" is a simple story (and a good way to work my son and his friends into the book), but it could be the most important story you ever read if you are interested in the investment "markets." For there is very little difference between the marble market and the more sophisticated markets of the world. The marble-market pattern was repeated over and over again in the 1980s— in real estate, gold, oil, bonds, and stocks. And I feel safe in predicting that it will continue to repeat itself throughout the rest of our history here on earth.

As we look at the various avenues of investment, and as you consider how and where to invest your money, think about the marble market at Central Elementary.

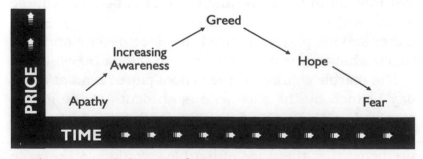

The ups and downs of an investment

6

Saving Without Market Risk

*Make all you can, save all you can,
give all you can.*

John Wesley

SPEND SOME TIME READING the books of Leviticus and Deuteronomy and you'll notice that the lending of money was recognized as a legitimate means of caring for God's children. These Scripture passages offer instructions about the proper lending of money, and logic suggests that there must have been rules for proper borrowing too. As we've seen, the Christian community has dealt with the word "proper" as it pertains to lending and borrowing for thousands of years, but many Christians today seem to be rejecting debt (i.e., borrowing) altogether rather than risk its abuses. Yet many of those same persons pay little attention to their own lending practices.

What I would like to do is put both into a proper balance so you can see how this particular financial activity can—and should—be beneficial for both borrower and lender.

Saving Versus Investing

We put the first money we accumulate into short-term deposits. Which is just another way of saying that we make a short-term loan to a financial institution—a short-term loan that we can get back whenever we want or need it.

Other than access to our money, the attraction of these investments (more properly called "savings") is safety. Such short-term deposits are not subject to the ups and downs of the stock, bond, and real estate markets, and they are insured by government affiliated agencies.[1]

---

1 Not all financial institutions are covered by these federal agencies. Unless you're a very knowledgeable investor, I suggest you stay with those that are.

The attraction of short-term investments (savings) is safety.

Historically the stock, bond, and real estate markets have provided superior long-term results, but I recommend that you invest a reasonable amount of money in short-term, guaranteed accounts. There are three reasons for this.

First, you can count on these deposits if you have an emergency or a major purchase, and we all need ready access to a lump sum of money at some time. Younger families need the buffer of about three months' living expenses, and retirees usually require more because of potential medical expenses. Six months' to a year's expenses would be a good guideline for the latter. Investors also need access to ready money to take advantage of new opportunities that may arise.

Second, even an optimist has to acknowledge that difficult periods arise from time to time. Some guaranteed money in short-term deposits at very solid institutions can provide a cushion against these periods.

And third, when used properly, this type of money can assist your neighbor.

Checking accounts, savings accounts, or money market funds at a bank or credit union are simply short-term loans to that institution. These typically have some form of the government's assurance.

Sums invested in a money market fund at an investment firm are usually used as short-term loans to large corporations. These are not insured but have an excellent record of safety, and they usually pay a little more than funds at banks because they involve a bit more risk—a prudent risk, in my opinion. Use the most convenient fund unless rates vary considerably or you desire to invest for ethical reasons.

Certificate of deposits (CDs) are loans to a bank for a longer period—from three months to several years—that you get back at maturity. These normally pay more than the others we've discussed because they tie up your money for a period of time and can be loaned by the institution for longer terms (you can withdraw money, but must pay a penalty). CDs are insured by federal agencies and are a particularly good place to put money when you anticipate an expense down the road.

Potential Problems

As with all investments, short-term deposits do have their disadvantages. First, they are fully taxable; and second, the income is unpredictable from year to year. If you are in one of the higher tax brackets or need dependable income, you shouldn't invest more than necessary in these areas.

Also, the government guarantee of banking deposits entices many to forget about the stability of the borrower (remember, this is money *you* are lending to the financial institution). This is not without its own risks. For example, if a bank collapses and is taken over by another bank, your certificate of deposit can be canceled.

I've had clients who had 10-year CDs at 14% canceled when their financial institutions failed. They then had to reinvest the returned money at 8%. Though they didn't lose principal, the loss of the *higher future income* played havoc with their budgeting process. This could be particularly painful if you are counting on that income during difficult economic periods (the very times when more marginal institutions tend to fail).

125

Types of Short-Term Deposits
Checking accounts
Savings accounts
Money market funds
Certificates of deposit

Value of Short-Term Deposits	Disadvantages to Short-term Deposits
1. Ready access to cash for emergencies and major purchases.	*1.* They are fully taxable.
2. Cushion against difficult times.	**2.** Income is unpredictable from year to year.
3. To provide assistance for your neighbor.	**3.** Risk of bank collapse.

Your best guarantee is to stay with a solid institution. One way to do that is to find a bank or savings and loan whose stock is traded publicly. That way you can get audited reports from any investment firm and watch the value of its stock for signs of trouble. It may also be possible to obtain an analyst's review that tells what the institution does with deposits. Another option is to deal with a local institution whose *activities*, as opposed to people, you know very well. Remember, the higher the promised return, the higher the risk— even though that risk may appear relatively small, it is still a risk.

Saving with Investment Firms

Investment firms offer CDs by simply sending your money on to banks or savings and loans. Normally, the financial institution pays the investment firm a commission so you don't have to, the interest rates are competitive, and the certificates are insured. The value goes up and down depending on interest rates. Theoretically this is an advantage in falling interest rate periods, but may be a disadvantage during rising interest rate periods. There is usually no preset penalty for early withdrawal; you simply sell the certificate to someone else at the prevailing price. This liquidity provision is not an ironclad one, of course, as a buyer must be found.

Investment firms offer CDs with up to 10-year maturities. This can be an advantage if you want to lock in current rates for an extended period of time. Some firms do a better job than others in evaluating the stability of the institution recommended. Do your own homework, especially if investing for a longer period of time. The minimum deposit is typically $1,000.

Investment firms also offer some certificates that most banks don't. Called "zero-coupon" certificates, these don't pay out interest on a regular basis. They just compound and mature at a multiple of what you invested. These are good for the qualified plans discussed earlier and for gifting to children. However, I don't recommend that you invest in these if you may need money back before maturity. The value before maturity can fluctuate widely. The primary advantage is that any interest earned compounds at the same rate as your original deposit. The minimum deposit can be as low as a few hundred dollars.

Ethical Questions

All these investments involve ethical considerations. For example, I have clients who believe that many welfare payments and a considerable amount of our defense spending are simply a government transfer of their tax dollars to others in our society. Surprisingly, many of these same clients don't think twice about sending their money all over America to institutions that are already in, or rapidly approaching, bankruptcy—simply because they pay an extra percent. In other words, they knowingly count on the U.S. taxpayer to subsidize their high returns through the government's insurance funds. Something to think about, right?

Some investors knowingly count on the U.S. taxpayer to subsidize their high returns through the government's insurance funds.

While many banking institutions could operate more efficiently and increase their interest rates, I've found that many pay more on their deposits by depleting the dollars invested by the institution's shareholders, or the dollars collected by the government's insurance funds, or eventually by charging the taxpayers themselves (when the FSLIC fund is depleted). By insisting on the highest rates we may unwittingly prosper at the expense of our neighbors, through even the most conservative investments.

This is just one example of the fact that most of us don't know what our bankers do with our deposits. (They don't really lock our money up behind vault doors until we need it again!)

Most of us don't know what our bankers do with our deposits.

I personally gave very little thought to all this until I began my search for meaning and understanding. I chose my bank because it was solid and had a reputation for being well-run and because I really liked the people at the local branch (and I still do). But I have moved a little money recently—certainly not all of it, since my bank does do some admirable work—after discovering that I didn't agree with all the things they used my deposits for.

Credit cards, for example. Many people want these little pieces of plastic. They offer a legitimate convenience, which I personally appreciate, so I carry some myself. But I also get three or four unsolicited, special offerings of new cards each week since I "have been judged to be a credit-worthy borrower" by someone I have yet to meet. (This person may or may not understand that this "preferred" credit rating might have resulted because I don't actually use the credit feature of the cards I already have.) Some of these companies actually take the trouble to call me at home (usually at dinnertime) with special offerings, promising that "the card" will make travel to exotic places and the good life available to me.

129

Actually, I seriously doubt whether anyone is better off just because they have a pocket full of credit cards. In fact, it could be just the opposite. These institutions offer this level of service not because they care about me personally, but because the credit card business is a very profitable one for the banks.

"Nowadays, many financial institutions are getting just as addicted to issuing credit cards as some people are to overusing them. They are bedazzled by the cards' profit potential: The 2 1/2% to 3% that many issuers earn on their card debt outstanding is mighty alluring to bankers who are doing well to chalk up a 1% return on total assets," reported *The Wall Street Journal* in May 1989.

A recent study by two universities concluded that 80% of the personal bankruptcies they studied could have been avoided had the financial institutions involved been more selective in their lending practices.[2] The study concluded that the institutions made the loans because the interest rates charged on the consumer loans were high enough to offset the losses of the bankruptcies. The results to the borrowers seem a bit more difficult to justify, of course.

There's a fine line between responsible lending to those in need and abusive lending to the overextended. Credit card institutions serve a useful role in today's society, and they have an obligation to their shareholders and society in general to remain solidly profitable. But they need to be more selective in their lending practices for consumer items. If they are not, they can draw valuable deposits away from essential business development and housing.

---

2 A joint study by the University of Pennsylvania and the University of Texas in Austin, reported in *The Wall Street Journal* (29 November 1989).

Because of this, I have decided that I can't express concern about the effect of credit cards on my younger neighbors yet continue to benefit by financing the card debt with my deposits. Some banks can pay the highest rates on CDs only because they use the money to make credit card loans that charge extremely high rates. If I express concern about credit card debt but continue to place my deposits with those actively engaged in promoting it, my money will speak louder than my words in shaping our world.

In commenting on how banks are changing the way they use our deposits, *Forbes* states that "as recently as the mid-1950s, Citibank put more of its depositors' money into Treasury securities than it did into loans." And another leading service reports, "By 1993, the bank's aggressive agenda calls for it to have 20% of all the credit card sales in the U.S."

Now don't get me wrong. Citibank does some admirable work (they supplied the mortgage money that put the roof over my family), and they aren't fully responsible for funding our nation's deficits. I only use them as an example because they are a highly visible, readily identifiable target (and because I recently noticed them promoting their credit cards to *college sophomores* on the campus of my alma mater. I don't think it's puritanical to raise ethical questions about the practice of encouraging college sophomores to enjoy "concerts" and "sporting events" at 19% interest rates.) But I do wish Citibank and similar institutions would be aware of the potential problems their business plans hold for all our citizens. My own awareness, as well as where I direct my money, might encourage that.

I also have doubts about what are commonly called "teaser" mortgage rates. Many young people risk getting in over their heads because they are lured by these creative mortgages which promise low first-year interest rates—rates that will certainly increase in the second and subsequent years. Banks and savings and loans promote these teaser mortgages because they believe people want them—and because they seem necessary in today's competitive environment. But in the interests of younger home buyers, they should tone down these promotions. If enough people, starting with me, move their money, maybe they'll begin to get the message. Especially if I mention why I'm withdrawing the money.

I have also stopped recommending some CDs offered through investment firms because the institutions these firms represent use the deposits to purchase junk bonds. I can't express concern about the possible dangers this form of excessive lending poses to society if I continue to finance them indirectly just because the certificates are federally insured and pay a higher rate. (Some banks that do not use investment firms to gather deposits also buy a lot of junk bonds. And a recent report indicated that the banks had made about $250 billion of these loans directly through what are known as "highly leveraged transactions," the banks' equivalent of junk-bond lending).

As a result of all this, I have established a rule-of-thumb formula: I watch how many ads for teaser mortgages, consumer loans, and credit card loans my bank distributes. The more they distribute, the more money I move; the more junk bonds they own and the more highly leveraged transactions they provide, the more money I move. (Thankfully, my bank does relatively little of this.)

I move this money to institutions that as far as I can determine operate on the principle that far too many loans are made solely for the wants of the borrower and based on the ability of the borrower to repay, rather than basing loans on the need and character of the borrower. These institutions aren't charities; they are insured, healthy, profitable establishments that pay competitive rates on deposits. For example, a growing number of banks and credit unions (often called "community development" organizations) will only use my deposit to provide responsible loans to low-income and minority households in our inner cities, in Appalachian areas, and on Indian reservations. In this way my deposit helps people buy homes, start businesses, and educate children. Also, there are programs that will use my money to make loans to the disadvantaged who want to start a cottage business.

I personally believe that these programs produce results that would warm the heart of the most cynical investor around. Several of these institutions are listed in the resource center at the end of the book, and I urge you to write for further information about them. Many try to provide modest blessings for the "meek and poor" of this earth, and most accept modest-sized deposits and retirement plans such as IRAs.

Do your bank a favor, too, and let them know about such programs and how they can be a profitable alternative to the excessive overseas, condominium, oil, credit card, and consumer lending some have pursued. Estab-

---

Would you know a junk bond if you met one?

As a result of the financial scene during the 1980s, "junk bond" has become a household word, although many may not know exactly what the term means.

A "junk" or "high yield" bond is a very aggressive loan to a corporation. Frequently these bonds are backed by few assets or earnings, because essentially they are loans to companies very heavily loaded with debt. For more information about these, see chapter 7.

---

lishing such programs might make depositors more comfortable doing business with them. When the resources of our world are allocated in an ethical manner, everyone wins—banks, depositors, and needy borrowers.

Insurance Company Contracts

Along with money market funds and bank deposits there is a third place where we can invest our money without being subject to market fluctuations, and that is with insurance companies. These are longer-term deposits offering a company guarantee and tax advantages, as opposed to the government guarantee offered by a bank or savings and loan. Insurance companies offer a range of investment choices, illustrated by the graph below.

Moving from left to right on the chart, the first type of investment is a "term" insurance policy. This is a guaranteed death benefit, with no savings built in. Next is "whole life," which is mostly death benefit, but offers some investment feature.

Next comes "universal life," offering a balance of protection and savings (the amount of savings in whole life and universal depends on the contract, the company, and the general level of interest rates). With

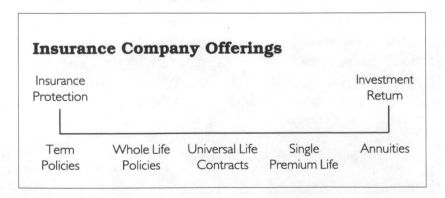

Insurance Company Offerings

Insurance Protection				Investment Return
Term Policies	Whole Life Policies	Universal Life Contracts	Single Premium Life	Annuities

"single premium life" the percentage of savings begins to outweigh the protection. And finally comes the "annuity," which offers only investment return, no insurance.

Those who consider insurance contracts a bad investment have usually bought those on the left of the graph, which are not really meant to be investments (although many have certainly been sold that way by ambitious but unfocused salespersons). These are designed specifically as protection for dependents who lose a provider.

During the early 1980s Americans became more aware of investment options, and one area this affected greatly was insurance contracts. Combined with the high, short-term interest rates of the period, this began to make the policies in the middle appear more attractive. The ones on the right have been popular for many years with knowledgeable, but conservative, investors.

Fixed Annuities

A fixed annuity can be described as a CD from an insurance company that is taxed much like an IRA. The company, rather than the government, guarantees your money against fluctuation or loss, and you receive a stated interest rate. Normally you don't pay a commission to your agent, who is paid by the insurance company.

Annuities are usually used as savings for retirement since, like an IRA, there is a federal tax penalty for money withdrawn before age 59 1/2. Interest earned on annuities is not taxed until the money is withdrawn, which makes them a natural for investors in their peak earning and tax years who are anticipating retirement, at which point income and taxes will probably drop.

An annuity can actually be viewed as two investments. The period from deposit until withdrawal is

135

called the "accumulation period." At some point in time, often at retirement, the investor *can* begin what is called the "annuitization period," when the company begins sending a monthly or quarterly check.

If you enter the annuitization period, the company looks at the size of your account and the average mortality figures for someone your age. They then determine how much they can send you each month over the rest of your lifetime. Since you aren't taking all your money out at this point, they assume your deposit will continue to earn interest; and since they are arranging a regular check for you, they have to establish a set interest rate. They do not know where interest rates will be over the coming years, so they generally make a pretty conservative assumption about how much interest they should credit you with each year.

For this reason I suggest that you might prefer to take what's called "partial withdrawals." (This is especially true if you think interest rates will tend higher over the years.) This means you write the company once a year and ask for one large check rather than having the company automatically send a monthly check.

This way you avoid establishing the annuitization period, during which money can't be surrendered from the company, and continue the accumulation period, which does allow the surrendering of the contract. In doing this, you have to make some assumptions about interest rates, and you might want to evaluate the company's assumed interest rate (you'll need a financial calculator), but generally I've found partial withdrawals the most efficient means for taking earnings from an insurance company. And your deposit stands a better chance of earning a competitive rate from year to year.

If you do decide to annuitize, you should understand that even though the entire amount you have accumulated may not be paid out to you before you die, there is usually nothing paid to your heirs. Some contracts offer a "period certain," which means a minimum number of payments will be made to you *or* your heirs, but I usually avoid these too. Taking partial withdrawals assures that your heirs will get anything you haven't taken out. (Notice: Most companies require some form of annuitization at an advanced age. Check details before buying.)

Single Premium Life Contracts

Single premium life is an annuity with a small amount of life insurance attached. By adding this insurance you can avoid income tax on the interest earned if you do not withdraw it but leave it for your heirs.

Single premium contracts are best suited for older investors who seek guaranteed, tax-advantaged returns and who do not need the interest and will probably pass it on to their heirs. A good rule of thumb is to buy an annuity if you plan to spend your interest, and buy a single premium life if you plan to pass it on to children.

Universal Life

When Congress recently changed the rules on single premium life (you used to be able to take the interest out tax-free for your own use), many companies began promoting "universal life" as an alternative. Variations of these policies have been around for years and were generally regarded as superior to whole life contracts as investment vehicles during the high interest rate period of the early 1980s. Today they offer fairly competitive

137

rates and an opportunity to withdraw savings on a tax-free basis.

As investments, these policies are difficult to evaluate. Different companies offer contracts with different balances of protection and investment return, so I know of no easy way to find a good contract. What I do is call two or three companies I respect and compare offerings. Because of the larger amounts of insurance protection, these are usually effective investment vehicles only if you pay into them for ten years or more.

Whole Life Contracts

As interest rates soared during the 1980s, whole life policies were much maligned. Because insurance companies had not always shared the wealth with policy holders as they could have over the years, many agents used that fact in selling their more competitive versions. This increased competition has forced most companies to be more generous in their whole life policies, which combined with the drop in interest rates has once more made whole life competitive with some of the newer policies.

Variable Annuities

Variable annuities do not guarantee a fixed interest rate or your principal, but are essentially mutual funds (which will be explained later). The return you receive depends on the performance of the fund you choose. Therefore, the key to variable annuities is finding a fund manager who has demonstrated an ability to manage money—not the insurance company with the strongest financials. But should two managers under consideration appear comparable, choose the contract offered by the strongest company. *Always choose a solid company.*

Variables offer two advantages over regular mutual funds. First, they are tax-deferred investments, which means you can move within the several funds available in the contract and can accumulate dividends and interest without having to pay current income taxes. Given the potential returns (and risks) of the markets, this makes them attractive to more sophisticated, higher-bracket investors. Second, most variable annuities offer a money-back guarantee in the form of a death benefit.

For example, you could invest $10,000 in a stock fund and watch it decline to $5,000 in a market crash. However, if this were invested in a fund within an annuity and the market fell, the company would still pay your heirs your original $10,000 if the policy were in force when you died. Since there is no free lunch, this feature costs about 1/2 of 1% each year in addition to regular management fees, but it may be worth the price if you worry about the ups and downs of the market. This feature also makes variables attractive to some pension plans and those who desire performance but need to be more conservative.

Some variable annuities allow minimum initial investments of $500, and much smaller subsequent investments.

Variable Life

Variable life contracts can be viewed as variable annuities with a little bit of insurance attached. This insurance guarantees your heirs more than you invested, but more importantly, it turns the money your heirs receive at your death into tax-free dollars. Variable life contracts are normally considered by wealthier, more sophisticated investors who are simply building their estate for their heirs. Again, the first criterion is the merits of the fund manager, and the second is the financials of the insurance company.

Minimum investment is usually $5,000.

Consumer Tips for Variables

Variable contracts offer significant advantages to some investors, and you do pay for some of these advantages. Most policies carry between 1 1/2% and 2 1/2% in annual fees.

A top stock fund manager can overcome this, but I question whether a bond fund manager or money market fund manager can. Therefore I usually recommend variable contracts for those seeking aggressive returns through the stock market. The death benefit, which guarantees a return of your money or a positive return on your money, makes them a logical choice for aggressive money that also seeks a minimal guarantee. They are one of the few ways to legitimately insure a common stock portfolio.

Funds within variable contracts are evaluated periodically by independent companies. Lipper Analytical Services is one I happen to use. The Standard and Poor's Stock Guide you see on most brokers' desks also reports on several variable managers. If you are considering a variable contract, I suggest that you ask for a recent report.

Past performance doesn't guarantee future results, nor does it measure the risks taken by the manager, but it is worth looking at. Some policies offer a real estate fund in addition to the typical stock, bond, and money market choices.

Consumer Tips for Fixed Contracts

The first practical consideration when investing in guaranteed, fixed contracts is to choose a company that is as safe as possible. You can do that by making sure the company has an A+ rating from a company called A.M. Best, the organization that is the most widely accepted authority on the subject.

Some advisors say an A rating is sufficient, but I prefer to stay with A+. I also like to stay with companies at least fifty years old. Some young companies who have A+ ratings have invested heavily in junk bonds and haven't been through hard times yet. (I make exceptions to these rating and longevity rules occasionally due to a specific need, but you will be reasonably certain to stay out of trouble if you consider only companies that meet these two criteria and avoid heavy investing in junk bonds.) An alternative approach is to check the rating from Moody's or Standard and Poor's. An AAA or AA rating from either of these services is highly encouraging.

Some large, well-known companies issue contracts through subsidiary companies. I suggest avoiding these unless the subsidiary meets the standards mentioned. I haven't been convinced yet that these parent companies back the contracts issued by their subsidiaries. They should put the name of the parent company on the contract (not just on the sales brochure) if the assets of the parent company are backing them.

We don't usually worry about the ability of insurance companies to come through with a substantial amount should our house burn, our car get wrecked, should we need an operation or die. However, if you write a check for $10,000 for an annuity, you might be a bit more concerned about the ability of the company to keep the contract. That may be well and good, because I believe there are problems brewing in the insurance industry, and recent practices by several companies remind me of those at some savings and loans a few years ago. Therefore, it is important to stay with very solid companies.

Since fixed contracts are usually used for retirement or to pass assets on to heirs, you are establishing a long-term relationship with any company you choose. But should your company not remain competitive or financially solid, you should be aware that you can usually move contracts from one company to another without triggering income taxes on past earnings. This is called a "1035 Exchange" and any experienced agent can help you with it. Before doing so, however, be sure to weigh any company penalties and the loss of any benefits older contracts were afforded.

And just a few last reminders: 1) Be skeptical of "projections" that aren't guaranteed, as they can be a bit rosy about the future. 2) Most insurance contracts avoid probate if a beneficiary is named, which can get your money dispersed to your heirs more quickly and at less cost. 3) Check an AM Best report and/or a rating from the other services, and always question any company with sizable junk bond holdings. 4) Make sure you're dealing with the parent company when comparing policies.

Ethical Considerations

While various sales practices of insurance companies can certainly be cause for ethical dilemmas and debate, I have found relatively few ethical problems in the use of money within the better companies. They tend to make long-term, conservative investments, finance and own very large real estate projects such as shopping centers and office buildings, and they buy tremendous quantities of high-grade bonds and common stocks. Certainly I would like to discover a high quality company that would dedicate my deposit to socially responsible areas, but at this point I am not aware of any (although some church denominations operate insurance companies for their clergy and members). Until

I find one, I will live with their generally conservative philosophies.

Guaranteed insurance contracts offer the conservative investor safety and tax benefits. Variable contracts offer long-term, tax-advantaged accumulation. They are best used for money you are putting away for retirement or for your heirs, and they offer valuable estate planning benefits since they can avoid probate. Although they are not always the most productive investments, I have had fewer complaints about them than with any other investment.

Even more than with most investment decisions, the important thing to consider with insurance is what it is you really want. Are you looking for protection or return? guarantees or variable performance? short-term or long-term results?

When dealing with agents and brokers, embrace skepticism and avoid cynicism. And remember: The higher the return promised, the higher the risk.

7

Investing for Stable Income (Bonds)

THE INVESTMENTS DISCUSSED IN the previous chapter, except the variable ones, keep the value of your money stable but allow your income to go up and down. Bonds do the opposite. They keep your income predictable but allow the value to go up and down until the bonds reach maturity. They should therefore be considered by retirees, pension plans, and others who seek a steady, predictable income.

Steady, predictable income can be an advantage. For example, when 6-month CDs were paying over 16% in the early 1980s, 20-year Treasury bonds paid around 15%. You could have bought a bond and assured yourself of a 15% income, guaranteed by the U.S. government, for 20 years to come. Your income would not have dropped as interest rates dropped. (The bonds appeared to offer less because the interest rate risk was less— but would have paid more.)

But steady, predictable income can also be a disadvantage. In 1986 when CDs were paying a little over 6%, many of my clients switched to government bonds paying 8%. Now interest rates are rising even as this is being written, but their incomes are not rising. They are locked into the 8% rate for years to come. (Again, the CDs paid less because the interest rate risk was less.)

Often the lowest paying investment provides the greatest return in the long run.

My point is that you should avoid following the crowd. Millions chase the highest interest rate, and in doing so, they simply chase the highest risk. It's a very, very difficult thing to do— it goes against everything in our human nature—but most people should consider the lowest paying investment. In the long run, it could provide the greatest return. You simply can't chase the highest rates without taking the highest risks. And you'll seldom profit by assuming the highest risks.

The Safety Factor

Bonds are simply long-term loans. Basically you loan your money to the United States government by buying Treasury bonds; to many home buyers, students, farmers, and others by buying government agency bonds; to city and state governments by buying municipal bonds; and to corporations by buying corporate bonds. Investors looking for the safest taxable income should look at Treasury and agency bonds. Investors who need income without additional federal income taxes should look at municipal bonds. Investors who seek higher taxable income than that offered by government bonds should consider corporate bonds.

Credit worthiness is not a major consideration with government bonds. They generally offer the highest guarantee of your money and interest that is available (remember, the government is the only borrower that can print its own money). Municipals and corporates usually do not offer government guarantees. For this reason, they are evaluated by rating services that provide guidelines about their credit standing.

The government is the only borrower that can print its own money.

Moody's and Standard and Poor's (S&P) are the two most widely quoted rating services. The highest rating is AAA (this designation varies slightly with the different services). The next highest is AA, and the next, A. There are additional ratings for lower quality bonds but I won't discuss them because I don't want to encourage you to consider them, even though they promise higher interest. Most investors should consider only AAA or AA. Remember . . . *the higher the return promised, the higher the risk (of default).*

Very conservative municipal bond investors should also consider "insured bonds," which are guaranteed by the issuer and doubly guaranteed by insurance organizations, in case anything happens to the issuer. After being insured, these bonds usually get an AAA rating, and you will normally lose less than 1/2% interest to be insured. Many investors will find it worth that to sleep better at night. (Notice, the insurance does not protect you against the ups and downs of your money until maturity; it simply guarantees your interest payments and *value at maturity.*)

Controlling Risk

If you cash in any type of bond before maturity, you will make money or lose money according to which way interest rates have moved since you bought your bond. To understand this, imagine that you bought one of the 15% Treasury bonds available in the early 1980s. It's now eight years later and you want to sell it to another investor because you need the money. Interest rates are much lower, so the investor is willing to pay you a nice profit just to get your bond which will still pay him 15% until it matures years from now. Of course, if today's interest rates were 25%, he wouldn't want your bond

149

paying 15% *unless* you sold it to him at a low price and took a loss.

The price of your bond will normally move in the opposite direction from interest rates. The more interest rates move, the larger the gains or losses. And longer maturity bonds normally move more than shorter maturity bonds. Most investors buy 20 to 30 year bonds because they pay a little more than others, but it might be wiser to invest some of your money in 5 to 7 year bonds in case you need to cash them in. However, all these concerns can be avoided if you simply hold your bonds to maturity. Remember . . . *the higher the return, the higher the risk (of market fluctuation).*

I find it interesting that the Old Testament encourages us not to lend money for more than seven years. Not a bad guideline for most of us even today.

BONDS	
Treasury bonds:	Loans to U.S. government
Government agency bonds:	Loans to home buyers, students, farmers, and others
Municipal bonds:	Loans to city and state governments
Corporate bonds:	Loans to corporations

RETURNS	
Safest taxable loans:	Treasury and agency bonds
Loans without additional federal income taxes:	Municipal bonds
Loans for the highest taxable income:	Corporate bonds

Some government and municipal bonds are backed by mortgages. Government National Mortgage Association bonds ("Ginnie Maes"), for example, are government bonds which pool your investment money with that of others and then make loans to people buying homes. These pay more interest than other government bonds and pay monthly, and these two features encourage many people to look at them. They are great investments IF you buy the right ones.

The major problem with any mortgage-backed bond is that home owners can return your money at any time by refinancing their mortgages. (A minor problem is that they return part of your original loan as a principal repayment each month and you have to make sure you don't spend it.) Many Ginnie Mae owners have been disappointed because they bought bonds backed by mortgages as high as 16% in the early 1980s. When the rates fell, the home owners refinanced those mortgages and took out new ones at the lower rates. Thus, the Ginnie Mae owners got their money back and had to reinvest at a lower rate. Investors could have avoided this by buying bonds backed by 8% and 9% mortgages or even lower, which were available for substantial discounts, meaning that their returns were only slightly lower than the 16% bonds. Instead, most investors wanted the very highest government-guaranteed interest possible. Remember . . . *the higher the return promised, the higher the risk (of refinancing).*

Taxable or Tax-Free?

Investors in the 28% and 33% tax brackets need to pay particular attention to the "after-tax" return of their investments. A taxable investment paying 9% is only producing about 6% for you, with the other 3% going to the government. Tax-free bonds may pay only 7% when

151

taxable investments are paying 9% but you still make more for yourself. Those 15% tax-bracket investors should buy taxable investments, but the rest should do a quick calculation to see which is best.

Your Top Tax Bracket	Divide the Tax-Free Interest Rate by
28%	.72
33%	.67

For example, you are in the 33% bracket and are offered a tax-free bond paying 7%. How does it compare with a government bond paying 9% taxable? Simply divide 7 by .67 and you get 10.45%. The tax-free is just like owning a government bond paying 10.45%. Since the government bond you've been offered is only paying 9%, you would be better off with the tax-free bond. Remember . . . *the higher the return promised, the higher the risk (of being taxed).*

Zero-Coupon Bonds

Government, municipal, and corporate bonds also come in "zero-coupon" form. Like the CDs discussed in the previous chapter, they don't pay you regular interest checks but simply mature at a multiple of what you invested. These are wonderful for providing a certain number of dollars for a particular date in the future.

The problem with zero-coupon bonds is that they fluctuate widely in value until they reach maturity. Therefore, you should always plan to hold them until that date. The municipal and corporate zero-coupon bonds are usually rated just like regular bonds, and I recommend those rated AAA or AA by Moody's or S&P's.

How to Buy Bonds

Basically you can buy bonds three ways: individually, as unit investment trusts, and through mutual funds. There are advantages and disadvantages to each.

Individual Purchase

I recommend individual bonds to fairly knowledgeable investors who have enough money to buy several. You can simply call any investment firm or most banks and speak with a broker. Tell the broker what quality bond you prefer, how many, and what maturity. (For example, say "I want $10,000 of an AAA-rated, 7-year maturity, tax-free bond.") Be sure to explain that you're not simply looking for the highest interest rate possible. (That will shock most brokers, but it will make their day!) Individual municipal, agency, and corporate bonds generally require a minimum of about $5,000. Ginnie Maes usually require at least $15,000.

You have seven days to pay for the bonds and can usually do it by mail. The broker may not be able to send you the actual bonds after you buy them, since many bonds are simply computer entries (if this is important to you, be sure to ask). Commissions are built in and do not affect the interest rate quoted, and they range from 1% to 4% depending on the bond. Obviously, these are not investments to buy and sell often.

Most individual bonds (except Ginnie Maes) pay interest every six months.

Unit Investment Trusts

You may have seen ads on television for "Nuveen Unit Trusts." This is one brand name for what's called a unit investment trust. It's called that because a company chooses several different bonds, sends them to a trust department, and you buy units of them.

153

Trusts are convenient because they allow you to invest in $1,000 increments regardless of the type of bond you choose. The bonds in a trust are not bought and sold by the trust department so there is no management fee, but you will pay a commission to buy through a broker (from 1% to 4% depending on the trust). And since there is no management fee to earn, there is no such thing as a no-load unit trust without a commission. The trust pays interest monthly or quarterly since it has several bonds paying at different times. This income doesn't fluctuate because the bond portfolio is fixed.

An important advantage of a trust is that the price you can sell at before maturity is the same whether you sell one unit or a hundred. Ordinarily, individual bond buyers suffer if they have to sell small amounts of bonds ($25,000 or less). Trusts contain rated bonds or insured bonds as described earlier. You may not get the very best deal around with a trust, but you shouldn't get a bad one if you stay with a discerning broker. My clients have been happy with them over the years.

Mutual Funds

A mutual fund is simply a large pool of money from many investors. Professional managers look after this money, and their expertise costs about 1/4% to 1/2% of your income. Some funds invest in government bonds, some in corporate bonds, and some in municipal bonds. With a mutual fund you can buy smaller amounts of bonds and add to your investment when you wish.

Larger investors often use mutual funds too, since a few managers do a good job of consistently providing above-average returns. You can get a feel for their competency by checking the performance numbers in S&P's Stock Guide, Lipper Analytical Services, or the more in-depth Morningstar Report we'll discuss soon. *Please* avoid buying a fund just because it runs ads about being the top-rated fund for the past quarter or year. The manager may have been taking unusual risks to get that return. Check performance over a period of several years.

The income from mutual funds is relatively stable but not fixed. It won't fluctuate as much as short-term investments, but it can rise or fall if interest rates change sharply. The values of unit trusts and mutual funds change much like individual bonds do. They should only be considered as a true investment, not a short-term holding.

Don't buy a fund just because it runs ads about being the top-rated fund for the past quarter or year.

Load Funds

Mutual funds that invest in bonds come in three basic forms. A load fund is the type you buy from an investment firm, requiring a broker's commission that can run anywhere from 1% to 8% of your investment. The average on a bond fund is about 3% to 4%, paid only when you buy, not when you sell.

Some funds disclose their commissions and some do not, but I would be wary of brokers who take their time to assist you and don't get anything out of it, or appear not to. My father's favorite saying was, "A businessman who says he's not making a profit is either a fool or a liar." He didn't believe in doing business with either one.

155

A businessman who says he's not making a profit is either a fool or a liar.

Many Americans today are always looking for a bargain— at least they think they are. They only want help from someone who will work for nothing. Unfortunately, they ignore the fact that a hidden commission will probably be larger than a disclosed commission. Brokers who find good investments, service your account, monitor your investments for you, and help you during difficult market periods work for percentages many businesspersons wouldn't. I guarantee you'll pay more over the years in a fund hiding the commission than in one disclosing it. If you don't want to pay a broker, find a fund in *The Wall Street Journal, Money* magazine, or another financial publication and buy direct.

No-Load Funds

If you know what you're doing (notice that I didn't say "*think* you *might* know what you're doing"), you should buy no-load funds. These are marketed directly to investors and do not pay commissions to brokers, so you are obviously ahead of the game by saving a commission. Unfortunately that is not the only consideration. (See chapter 8 for further pitfalls in no-load funds. Please read them carefully.)

Morningstar's Mutual Fund Values analyzes many no-load funds. And the American Association of Individual Investors, a non-profit, educational group, publishes a superb guide to no-load funds called *The Individual Investor's Guide to No-Load Mutual Funds*. It can help you do your homework about a fund's long-term track record and is available for $19.95 by writing to the association: 625 North Michigan Avenue, Chicago, Illinois, 60611.

Closed-End Funds

Closed-end bond funds are not marketed by brokers or no-load mutual fund groups (except at the very beginning of their lives). For convenience, they are traded on one of the stock exchanges and can be purchased like a regular stock; however, they are still bonds.

Closed-end funds can be attractive for two reasons: First, they often sell for less than the true value of the bonds, which is like buying a fund with a negative commission. This is as close to a "free lunch" as you get in our business. Second, the fund manager can depend on a stable portfolio, since money doesn't come and go from this type of fund. This means you get a better and a more predictable income.

Wait for these funds to have a year's track record before buying them. They tend to drop in value immediately after being issued; and when they are first being marketed, they often promise more than they can deliver. Buying a fund that's at least a year old helps avoid both problems.

Additional Warnings

First, you don't want bond funds that use "options and futures" in their normal course of business. Theoretically it's possible for these to be used for your benefit, but I've found they are usually used just to hype the promised return. For this reason, funds carrying the word "plus" in their names and those promising more income than bonds in general should be subject to special scrutiny.

Second, two interest rates can be quoted for mutual funds. The "SEC Yield" is what can be advertised. The

157

"distribution rate" is what a broker can tell you over the phone. What you want is the "SEC Yield." It may be somewhat lower, but it's closer to the true yield, in my opinion.

The long and short of my advice is: avoid the above problems by buying bonds and mutual funds promising an average rate of return. You won't encounter most of the questionable practices around today unless you seek out the very highest paying investments. Remember . . . *the higher the promised return, the higher the risks (of being misled).*

High Yields . . . at High Costs?

"High yield" bonds (they're seldom called "high risk" bonds) or "junk bonds," issued by financially weaker companies and cities, promise a very high interest rate. Their high yields appear enticing, and there are legitimate opportunities, but these should be viewed skeptically. Personally I believe these bonds are entirely different animals from traditional bonds.[1]

Junk bonds issued by corporations are the highest paying bonds around and have therefore been very popular recently. Basically they were marketed by one particular firm during the 1980s— Drexel, Burnham, Lambert— but a federal indictment appears to be weakening their hold on the market, and other investment firms are seeking the business. This is important to know, because you are likely to be exposed to them as more and more of the larger firms begin to discuss their "merits."

---

1 During the writing and publishing of this book, many of the problems concerning the junk bond market became very evident. Because of that, this section can now be read more as an explanation than as a caution.

Essentially junk bonds exist because someone wants to put a little money down and buy a company. They want you to provide the rest of the money by buying a junk bond. If all goes well, they can make a lot of money and you'll get your interest. But if things go wrong, they'll lose a relatively small amount of money and you'll lose your interest and usually some principal as well. My personal opinion is that if you're going to take most of the risks of owning a company, then you should also take the returns of owning a company. These people can buy companies if they want to . . . just as long as they risk their own money and not mine.

My other objection to junk bond financing is that it appears to be a very expensive enterprise. During the federal indictment of DBL it was revealed that one employee was paid over $500,000,000 as an annual salary plus bonuses. Ultimately this money came from the commissions on bonds sold by the firm— paid for by the buyers of the bonds. For that amount we could have financed the staffing of a community development bank in every major city in America and would have done more good.

I don't doubt that junk bonds have done some good for people over the years, as the ads say. But the community development banks of the country could have rebuilt most of the inner cities of America with the money that has been channeled into junk bonds recently. Instead of trying, and often failing, to create mega-millionaires through leveraged buyouts, we could have created a lot of low-income housing and small businesses. It's simply a question of *how much good . . . for how many people . . . for how much money?*

Some people did make some money buying junk bonds during the 1980s, but it's difficult to measure how much of that was just because it was a decade when most things went pretty well in the business

159

world (some of those bonds are now showing definite problems). Most investors would have done substantially better, with no more risk, by buying a growth mutual fund or a blue-chip stock in an ethically managed company. Again, it's simply a question of *how much return . . . for how much risk?*

How will these bonds perform when the economy weakens? It's been estimated that 90% of all junk bonds have been issued during the past four years and have not been tested during difficult times. Invest a few minutes in the library with the 29 May 1989 *Barron's* and the article entitled "Ignorance Isn't Bliss" before investing money in junk bonds or high-yield mutual funds. It's an enlightening look at how few investors are really shown the many risks they're taking with these bonds.

There's an epidemic today, and it's called "ignoring risk in order to achieve the income we think we need." Recently a young friend who's a broker at a savings and loan tried to convince me that high-yield funds are the only solution for retirees needing income.

After some serious debate, he finally acknowledged that his strategy actually encouraged those least able to afford the risk to take the most. That mentality has closed the doors of many financial institutions in this country.

I work in Florida where we have a significant population of retirees on a fixed income, so I am well aware that many people will ignore these warnings about seeking high yields. To those who are thus tempted, I suggest: at least give yourself a fighting chance by buying medium grade (BBB, BB and B) bonds through an astutely managed and very diversified mutual fund. You'll have to give up the last 1% in yield with these medium-grade obligations but at least you'll avoid the real junk that's around.

Please understand that I thought long and hard before even including that last paragraph about what I consider a fairly prudent way to seek higher yields because *I don't want to suggest that I encourage that measure.* But I just had a client invest a substantial amount of money in a "high yield" fund rather than some AAA/AAA-rated, government guaranteed bonds I suggested. The fund quoted less than 2/10ths of 1% more in yield. I provided him with a lengthy article on the concerns of junk and a written disclaimer that he was taking action that was opposite my advice. He thought it was the thing to do anyway. So I realize that some of you will to do the same thing . . . just give yourself a chance by considering the above suggestion.

Money is always there.
Only the pockets change.

There is an old saying in our business that "the money is always there, only the pockets change." Today, I think it makes more sense than ever to put the money in pockets where it accomplishes some ethical objectives (there are usually fewer holes in these pockets anyway), as we'll soon see. I always found it difficult to buy junk bonds after evaluating the risks, but since I have truly been applying the principles of my faith and evaluating where the true benefits flow, I have found it impossible. I have decided I can no longer express concern about the concentration of wealth in this country while continuing to finance a leveraged buyout of a corporation for a mega-millionaire. Think about this as you make decisions about your bond money.

Deceiving Appearances

Bonds can be terrific investments, but I hope I have convinced you of the folly of simply chasing the highest interest rate quoted. This area more than any other is dominated by investors looking for "just a little higher rate." I've tried that myself and have been burned every time.

I've learned to be wary of a bond paying more than other bonds of similar quality and maturity. I once decided I couldn't go wrong with a government-guaranteed bond paying a tax-free return of 14%. Similar bonds were paying 13% and under at the time. It was the Washington Public Power Authority ("Whoops" for short) and the bond has caused me severe indigestion for years even though the ones I bought have paid off to date.

I've also learned to be wary of "special situations" that pay more than similar bonds. I put a lot of money in a mutual fund of government bonds managed by one of the world's largest institutions. It promised 1% more than government bonds were paying at the time, but seemed foolproof. It wasn't.

And I've learned to be wary of "special" bonds someone is "kind enough to let me in on." There are no well-kept secrets in the financial world. Thousands of mutual fund managers,

Beware of These Promises

. . .

"Just a little higher rate"

"A special situation"

"Value-added"

"Kind enough to let you in on a good deal"

"A good deal that's only available if you act now"

trust officers, pension plan managers, and professional investors are diligently looking for any "special" bonds that may exist. They trade about $100,000,000,000 worth of U.S. government bonds each day. The odds of them missing "a good deal" are slight.

Please believe me when I say that you get what you pay for in the bond market. The competition is fierce among bond brokers, and you'll undoubtedly get much more than you're looking for if you insist on the last 1/2%! It simply won't work.

Ethical Lending

Ethical considerations center on "What's the borrower doing with my money?" For example, many ethical government bond investors like to buy bonds from the Government National Mortgage Association. "Ginnie Maes" finance the purchase of homes for lower and moderate-income families. I am particularly attracted to the social merits of "mobile home Ginnie Maes," for they specifically finance what is often entry level housing for new homeowners or for the elderly. The Federal National Mortgage Association, "Fannie Mae," is an AAA-rated, quasi-governmental institution, which in essence guarantees your money if you want to make a conventional mortgage loan to someone buying a home. They also recently announced bonds that would allow lower-income, senior home buyers to free up some cash for living expenses. I personally hope bonds of this nature become more widely available and are considered by the ethical investor. They have strong social merits.

The Student Loan Marketing Association, "Sallie Maes," issues securities that finance loans to college and trade-school students. These are usually secured by student loans insured by state agencies or the government and are considered a high-quality issue. In

163

> **Before Investing
> Ask Your Broker**
>
> . . .
>
> "What's my return?"
>
> "What's my risk?"
>
> "How does it affect
> society?"

the past I have been concerned about how some of this money was used, but recent efforts to tighten regulations has me looking at these securities again.

"Farm Credit" bonds are agency bonds used to finance agricultural loans to farmers. Some of these borrowers engage in questionable labor practices, which can be a consideration for ethical investors; but the overall merit of lending to the average farmer who grows our food suggests these are worth your consideration.

Some municipal bonds offer opportunities for the ethical investor seeking tax-free income. For example, those issued to finance the building and operation of schools and those issued by local housing authorities to finance homes for low and moderate-income families. Some of these housing bonds have been AAA-rated and backed by Ginnie Maes lately, so you can achieve a nice tax-free return with superior quality. Pollution control revenue bonds (PCRs) are tax-free bonds issued to finance pollution control facilities, a good option for the environmentally aware investor in a high tax bracket.

Corporate bonds that finance the manufacture of weapons, nuclear power plants, or corporate activities that endanger a substantial number of jobs might be avoided by those with sincere ethical concerns. Most corporate bond buyers (and even some money market fund investors) apply many of the same ethical criteria as stock buyers. You should be on strong ethical ground with the bonds of a company whose stock is recommended by some of the leading ethical advisory services. You should, of course, subject these companies to regular analysis for safety and other areas of prudence.

Some ethical investing experts even avoid U.S. Treasury bonds because a large portion of their money finances military activities. While some people are willing to live with this fact, I personally have cut down on purchasing Treasury bonds because of the U.S. military expense and the fact that I believe Congress might come closer to balancing our budget if I don't contribute to financing its excesses (a special concern of mine). Admittedly, I buy a few since these bonds also finance social programs and I don't want to leave the country in a bind as we try to finance the government debt already incurred. It's a compromise I feel I can live with.

Lessons from the Past . . . for the Future

When I was growing up in Kentucky, there was one man who had a profound influence on me. This man asked little from life other than the opportunity to work hard six days a week and worship on the seventh. He was a man of modest means, living in an area not noted for its economic strength, but he always held out great hope for the future. His single greatest desire was to educate his three children in the ways of heaven and earth and assure them a future brighter than his own past.

The main source of income for this man and most of his relatives, friends, and neighbors was the growing of tobacco, and this income was very instrumental in en-

Lending to the neediest borrowers is sometimes the safest thing we can do with our money.

One thing that has intrigued me since I began my search is the discovery that lending to some of the neediest borrowers is often the safest thing I can do with my money. According to Marcia Stigum in her book *The Money Market,* this is because

Congress has periodically taken the position that for some groups of borrowers, the available supply of credit was too limited, too variable, or too expensive. In each instance remedy was Congress's to set up a federal agency charged with providing a dependable supply of credit at the lowest cost possible to these disadvantaged

abling him to send his children through college. One became an environmental attorney; one raised two of the most beautiful children imaginable; and one entered the investment community.

Of course, this man was my father.

Were he alive, I think Dad would like this book. But I also think he would ask two things of us as we consider its contents.

First, he would ask us to be slow to pass judgment.

My father believed in certain absolutes, and he lived by them. But he also knew that no one fully understands God's ultimate plan, and no one is perfect. We are all, as borrowers. Some federal agencies are owned and directed by the federal government, and their debt obligations are backed by the full faith and credit of the U.S. government. Others are federally sponsored but privately owned. The obligations of federally sponsored agencies presumably have de facto backing from the federal government . . . it is important to note that agency and federal debt differ sharply with respect to both source and character. Most Treasury debt is the result of government deficits, a true national debt. In contrast, agency debt is incurred to make loans, largely to credit worthy borrowers.[2]

Agency bonds lend my money to people I am concerned about, with a proper level of prudence and in a way I can live with politically. For me, that's a good combination.

---

2 Marcia Stigum, *The Money Market* (Homewood, Ill.: Dow Jones Irwin, 1978, 1983), 212.

Bill Moyers is fond of pointing out, "insider traders," using resources in self-centered ways in our own fashions.

And Dad would also remind us that when we make our investment decisions, we are not making simple portfolio decisions; we are making people decisions.

In the light of today's medical research, he'd probably agree that we need to grow less tobacco. But he would also argue that we could put the present taxes on tobacco products to good use by financing agricultural research that would allow his friends and neighbors to change crops and profitably engage in feeding the starving people on our planet. Or, if we need to cut back on the construction of military weapons, we could use the

Be sure to review all the alternatives available for this type of investing. For example, most people know that Ginnie Maes usually come with an average maturity of 12 years. Fewer know that they are also available in a 6-year version called a "midget." With the latter, you can lend to home buyers who need a hand, receive a government-guaranteed monthly check, avoid the longer-term lending I question, and get an attractive return. I believe more people would support this prudent, responsible type of lending if they knew about these and the other options available. In the resource center at the end of the book I've listed the ones I prefer.

There's no question that some bonds will promise higher interest than the ones I've suggested, but I've found that those with commendable social merits have enviable records of avoiding problems that appear with many higher-rate bonds. Also, it's important to remember that the stated interest rate on some bonds is more

---

available resources to finance clean, efficient mass transportation and thus employ potentially displaced workers.

In other words, many potentially "good" decisions we make about money also carry the possibility of "harming" someone. The world is an interconnected place. Ethical investing is not just a portfolio manager disagreeing with the president of a tobacco company.

As I've worked through my own ethical concerns, I've thought long and hard about what my father would think. And I've often heard him cautioning me about two things: In our efforts to create a better society through the way we invest our money, we must not let it be-

---

of a "promised possibility" than a guarantee. Ask your banker or broker the tough questions and weigh the answers according to social merit, safety, political concerns, and the return promised. If you do this, you'll put money in the right pockets . . . and find it's in your own best interest too.

come just another marketing gimmick to a culture already made cynical by recent investment and corporate practices. And we cannot let this effort become some kind of pseudo-holy, exclusive but ineffective investment club seeking "purity" in a complex world.

I think Dad would advocate awareness, education, and cooperation to find the right balance. Dad was pretty good at getting priorities straight.

8

Investing for Growth (Stocks)

Try not to become a man of success but rather try to become a man of value.

Albert Einstein

OWNING A BUSINESS IN AMERICA offers an opportunity for prosperity that few other ventures can match. Although there are risks involved, the rewards are proportionate. Indirectly, of course, anyone can "own" a business by investing in the stock market.

For many people, mentioning the stock market is the equivalent of saying "Take a trip to Las Vegas." Even our industry refers to the very best companies as "blue *chip.*" And this often uninformed fear is understandable. Speculators have turned the stock market into a very up-and-down affair if you just look at the short-term.

But it's long-term prosperity that should interest conservative investors. In the short-term, you incur risk by being *in* the stock market. In the long-term, you incur risk by being *out* of the stock market. Actually, short-term speculators can help us as long-term investors *if* we set the ground rules.

Well-run, financially sound businesses will continue to be of economic value despite the interference of Wall Street speculators, and this value will be reflected in stock prices over the long run. Notice that when the author of Ecclesiastes advised to "invest your money in foreign trade" he also added "and ONE OF THESE DAYS you will have a profit." Three thousand years later, the watchword is still the same: patience, patience, patience.

Why Bother?

Stocks have averaged about 10% return a year since before the Great Depression of the 1930s. That is approximately 6% more than the inflation rate. By comparison, Treasury bonds have averaged only about 1% more than the inflation rate. Stocks have returned about 25 times as much as short-term deposits such as

Treasury bills. And these are average figures. A well-chosen portfolio of stocks or a top mutual fund would have done even better. This outstanding performance is one reason I suggest we set our own ground rules to deal with the speculators, rather than simply abandoning this productive area to them.

Another is simply that corporations continue to be a major means of controlling wealth and producing goods, services, and jobs. As Christians, we can exert an important and vital influence if we have a part in the ownership of this wealth. Corporations are only groups of people engaged in business, and as people they are far from perfect. They have to deal with greed, in-

---

Reasons for Christians to Invest in the Stock Market

1. Outstanding performance over the long term.

2. Corporations are a major means of controlling wealth, producing goods, services, and jobs.

3. Exert a positive and ethical influence in this area.

Types of Investors	Types of Stocks
Speculators	Speculative
Traders	Growth
True Investors	Blue Chip
	Utilities

humanity, and exploitation of our world's resources. As owners, we can affect these powerful forces that affect our world. I believe that an awareness and exercise of ownership rights and responsibilities—that is, keeping an eye on corporate management—will provide a more positive influence than simply leaving both in the hands of those less concerned with ethical considerations.

Strategies

Our first strategy is to decide what sort of investors we want to be. Investors fall into three categories: speculators are those who hold their investments for a month or two; traders are those who hold their investments from three months to a year; and true investors are those who hold their investments for several years.

Any broker will tell you that everyone says they are investors. Yet it sometimes seems the only investments people own today are short-term trades that didn't work out—they "should have invested in something else" because their stocks aren't up after three months. If that's your mentality, you need to read a different book, stay out of the market, or find a professional trader to assist you. Before you do, however, think about why you are investing.

- *Are you investing to create a better world for yourself, your neighbors, and your children?*
- *Or, are you simply trying to make a fast buck in an easy manner?*

If your answer is the latter, I would urge you to review the words of Proverbs and Ecclesiastes that we discussed earlier. They'll tell you that you're heading for trouble.

Isaiah 28:16–17 clearly establishes a bedrock ethic of Christianity especially pertinent to owning and operating a business that produces goods and services. "I am placing in Zion a foundation that is firm and strong. In it I am putting a solid cornerstone on which are written the words, 'Faith that is firm is also patient.' Justice will be the measuring line for the foundation, and honesty will be its plumb line." Patience, justice, and honesty—not a fast buck or an easy deal—are the ideals of Christian endeavor.

Types of Stocks

Stocks can be divided into four categories: speculative, growth, blue chip, and utilities.

Speculative stocks represent ownership in companies just getting started or in businesses that are weak for some reason. I do not believe there is any reason for the average investor to even consider these; there are so many, many ways to go wrong with them. You can get speculative stocks from any broker, but "penny stock brokers" specialize in them. Avoid these.

Growth stocks represent ownership in sound companies that cover a limited geographical area or a small percentage of their total industry. In other words, these businesses offer considerable room for expansion, giving them the opportunity to grow. This means the value of the stock can grow much larger over the years, but this larger potential return is also accompanied by larger risk.

Growth stocks are usually considered by younger investors who have time to allow the companies to grow. If you are interested in this, I recommend investing in mutual funds that invest in these types of stocks, since they can buy a great diversity and monitor them closely for signs of trouble.

Blue chip stocks represent ownership in large and very solid companies. A good example would be IBM.

There is little risk of IBM going out of business. However, there is also little risk of IBM doubling its sales next year since it already sells to virtually everyone in America. Blue chip stocks increase sales in proportion to population increases and inflation factors. Many of these stocks can provide an income since they pay out some profits (dividends) rather than putting the money into new factories and stores, as growth companies do.

Blue chip stocks are most appropriate for more mature investors or conservative younger investors.

Utility stocks represent ownership of electricity, water, gas, and telephone companies, which are usually the most conservative companies around because they are monopolies. They do not have to worry about competition like even IBM does. These companies are not affected as much by economic conditions as they are by changes in interest rates. They do best during falling interest rate periods or stable interest rate periods. They do not normally perform well when interest rates are rising.

Utility stocks are for investors who have a particular interest in income, but want some growth too. This income has the ability to keep up with inflation over the years since it is not fixed. Utility companies can increase your income as they expand their areas of operation and increase utility bills. Stay with high quality companies, not just the ones paying the highest income. The latter are normally troubled.

The Problem of Timing

Most casual investors in the stock market make some universal mistakes (over and over again). For example, stocks are one of the few items in this world that get harder to buy as the price gets cheaper. Lots of people wanted them in September 1987 and wouldn't touch them in November 1987 when the crash marked them down by 30% and more. It is for this reason I suggest most people not try to "time" the market (that is, choose exactly the right time to buy or sell) but simply decide to invest a certain amount each year, regardless of how they feel about the health of the market.

If you do decide to time the market—and most people do, whether they realize it or not—it's essential that you separate yourself from the crowd. I have known for years that you always make money by doing the opposite of what others are doing (for example, selling in September 1987 and buying in November), but I still can't do it. There are unbelievable influences from the media and the financial services to go with the crowd. That's why I have adopted a buy-and-hold attitude for myself.

Timing the market creates a tremendous amount of stress. My firm has a very respected formula for getting in and out of the market, but brokers are always mad at the strategists because they can't predict each move nor the exact timing when they are right.

Another problem is that after you have decided which way the market is going, you then have to pick the stocks to buy or sell. *The Wall Street Journal* has begun evaluating the ability of the major investment firms to predict the general market, and another of their studies evaluates the firms that pick the best stocks. I recently noticed that the firm that was best at timing the market was considerably less successful at picking stocks.[1] I'm not sure what good it does anyone to predict that the market is going up if you put your money in stocks that don't go up with it. In other words, the time you spend analyzing the direction of the market is time you cannot spend analyzing your actual investment. And the

---

1 *The Wall Street Journal* (9 November 1989): C-1.

latter, in my opinion, is much more important and rewarding.

Even if you are very adept at market timing, the effort may or may not be that important. Two major mutual funds have done studies comparing gains from investing on the lowest day of the year and the highest day of the year over a long period of time. The returns were remarkably similar. The point is that most gains were produced simply by getting in *sometime*, not getting in at the best possible moment. What the funds didn't say, but what most brokers could tell you, is that most people who try to time their purchases would come closer to the highs than the lows.

Some market timers like to show how well you could do if you could somehow pick when to get in and out. They rarely show how bad you can hurt yourself if you aren't very, very good at it.

My friends at the Putnam Group of mutual funds like to provide the following example, based on a University of Michigan study. The strong stock market from 25 August 1982 to 25 August 1987 saw the Standard and Poor's 500 increase at an annual rate of 26.3% during those 1276 trading days. Had you been out of the market during the best 10 days of that period, your return would have declined to 18.3%. Had you been out during the top 40 days of the 1276, your return would have been 4.3%!

The few professionals I know who move in and out of the market effectively do not try to predict the future, but simply analyze whether stocks are a good value relative to bonds and money market funds. That's totally different from what most individuals do, and it requires years of experience and hours of work. If you're considering hiring someone who says he or she can do this, be sure to get an audited track record, because many who claim the ability actually cannot do it.

For most people the best approach to the stock market is to invest in proven growth mutual funds on a steady basis over many years. In doing this, you accept the fact that the funds will go down occasionally. The successful Pioneer Fund I mentioned earlier lost half their clients' money during the early 1930s as the Depression deepened. The fear that that could happen again—and it could—makes many investors nervous, so they avoid the market. But I would simply point out that while homes, farms, private businesses, and other assets were lost during the Depression, the fund not only endured, but also paid dividends throughout the period. And those who continued to invest on a steady basis are not complaining today.

If you are a person who finds it impossible to live with the long view in mind, stay with utilities or higher yielding, blue chip stocks that provide immediate returns through dividend payments. There are many ways to pick such stocks, but there's one I particularly like.

The Conservative-Contrarian Approach

A company called Value Line evaluates stocks on a weekly basis. You can find the service in most investment firms and libraries, or you can subscribe to it (see the resource center at the back of the book). They present one-page, concise reports on each company, telling what the company does, its finances, recent activities, and a history of stock price and dividends. They also rate the company's stock for "safety" and "timeliness" from a high of 1 to a low of 5.

Their "safety" rating largely reflects a company's financial strength. I love #1 rated companies and like #2 rated companies. These are the most solid companies in America, and they can be expected to weather the ups and downs of the economy.

Value Line's "timeliness" rating concerns the analyst's opinion of the stock's performance over the next twelve months. Here I love the #5 rated companies, like #4 rated companies, and occasionally buy a #3 rated company (yes, the lowest rated companies). I'm not concerned about what the stock does over the next few months. I am concerned about what it does over the next few years. But I want the best companies in America when others are willing to sell them cheap. This occurs when they have small problems that their financial strength and management should solve.

Analysts often say to sell during this period because everyone is interested in the short-term. That pushes the price of the stock down, and I can buy it! Find a sell opinion from most analysts on Wall Street and you'll find a stock that has probably already dropped in value. Find a sell on a high-quality company and you've often found a bargain.

Each week Value Line provides a convenient computer printout of all companies with a #1 or #2 safety rating. I only have to scan one or two pages for the stocks rated #3, #4, or #5 for timeliness (see sample on page 182). Then I can turn to the full page report, where I check the points illustrated on pages 184–85.

Using the Value Line Investment Survey

The front section of the survey (see page 182) contains a computer printout of all the conservative stocks ranked #1 or #2 for "safety." Scan the "timeliness" column for those stocks rated #3, #4, and preferably #5. You can then go to the page number of the full report (FPL Group is illustrated on page 185).

This selection method is for the conservative, patient investor. If you wish to invest for higher potential

The Thoughtful Christian's Guide to Investing

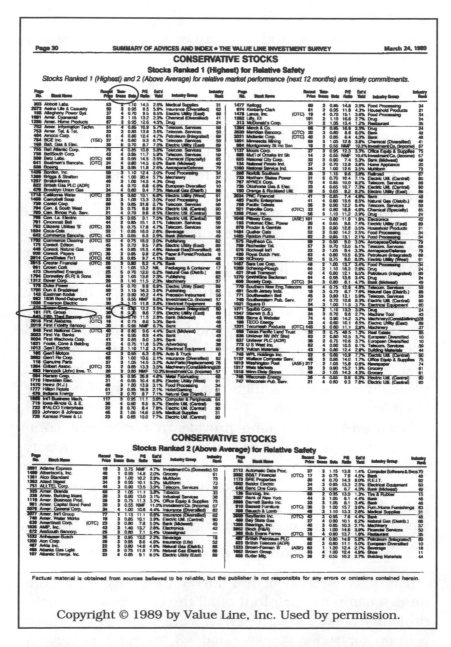

returns I suggest you choose a good growth mutual fund or find a good money manager.

I'm not saying the analyst is wrong to recommend selling a stock with 10% to 20% potential annual returns. That's his opinion *for the long-term.* But since most investors today are traders and want the short-term opinion, they often sell based on that. I can't keep them from trading, but there's no reason I shouldn't use it to advantage. This is why I maintain that you shouldn't concern yourself with Wall Street speculators. Set your own rules and allow them to help you by accommodating their desires to sell to you at lower prices.

This is a "contrarian" philosophy, and many successful investors use some form of it. Philip L. Carret, manager of the Pioneer Fund for fifty-five years, recently said, "I am a contrarian by nature, by conviction, and by long experience." John Templeton is another noted practitioner of the art. (Boomer and Justin, our marble makers, are just beginning to appreciate its benefits.) You can use any research department on the street—just scan their "sell" lists and compare them to S&P's quality ratings—but our Value-Line approach is relatively simple and available to most of us, regardless of investment firm.

Contrarian investing is not just buying what others do not want. It is buying the best companies at a time when few others want them. Also, you can't be contrarian and only buy stocks that have glowing research reports available. You have to concentrate on the long-term potential and the safety, but forget the short-term considerations. This requires a bit of "faith."

Contrarian investing is buying the best companies at a time when few others want them.

183

In the full-page report I check the following points:

❶ Confirm the timeliness and safety ratings.

❷ These are the high and low annual return projections for the stock for the longer term. FPL shows a high of 19% per year to a low of 13% per year projected by the analyst.

❸ The recent price of the stock.

❹ The highest level the stock has been in the last five years. This should be at least 10% to 20% above the current price. It's often far more.

❺ The dividend yield at the recent price. (Two numbers mean the analyst believes a dividend reduction is likely.)

❻ The company's business lines, address, and phone number.

❼ The analyst's discussion of current events at the company. Expect this to read somewhat negatively.

❽ The company's financial strength rating. It should be at least A.

There are usually enough 4-1 and 5-1 stocks around to fill a portfolio, but look at #2 safety stocks too. I actually buy an occasional #3, which is average for safety, but hesitate to recommend that for other people's money. If you buy a 4-1 and the rating changes to 5-1, just buy another 100 shares if the price has slipped a bit.

And remember, this is a lower risk strategy *for the patient.* Ask yourself how you'll feel after a year if the stock hasn't made money yet. If that will bother you, do one of four things: 1) tell your broker that your objectives are to trade (in which case, you should buy the

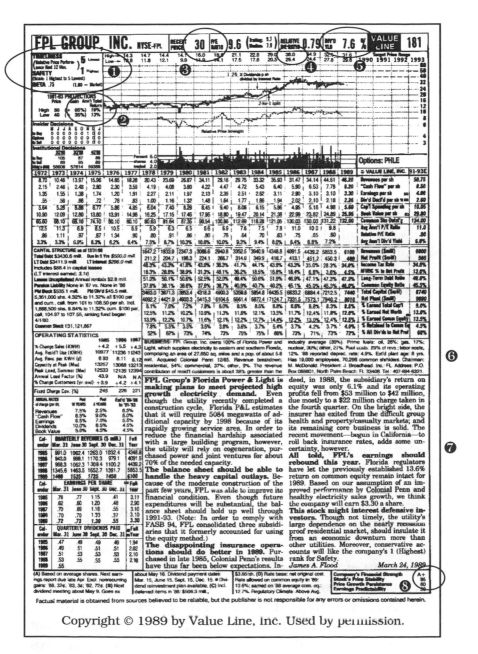

top-rated stocks and then plan to get out quickly); 2) buy bonds; 3) buy CDs; 4) buy the stocks when the analysts first raise their opinion on a #4 or #5 rated stock; or 5) buy a mutual fund.

Equity Mutual Funds

Mutual funds that invest in stocks come in the three varieties that bond funds do. You get a "load fund" from a broker, a "no-load" directly from some fund companies, and a "closed end" fund from one of the stock exchanges.

Few give as much self-serving advice as that given by load and no-load advocates. Brokers naturally favor load funds but often do little to earn their commission. Brokers should help select the appropriate fund, stay in touch with management (the fund may not tell you when the person actually managing your money is replaced), service your account, and help you stay with your fund for the long haul (assuming everything is going reasonably well). They are then worth a commission in my opinion. It is the "help you stay with your fund" advice which seems to be rare these days.

No-load advocates believe a commission saved is like money in the bank, and they point out that the average load fund has not performed any better than the average no-load over the years. They are right on both points. Unfortunately, that's obvious and like all obvious investment matters, it's not the whole story.

Commission charges are important considerations, but some load funds can save commissions as well as no-load funds. You don't have to pay a commission when you enter a no-load fund, but the fund still has to pay commissions when the manager buys and sells stocks on your behalf. This is important for you to understand, because there is a lot of what I call "hot money" in no-load funds today. This in itself creates several expenses for the funds' investors, and these can be rather significant. For example, the *Individual Investor's Guide to No-Load Funds* reports the Fidelity Value Fund, a no-load fund, has averaged over 350%

annual portfolio turnover from 1983 through 1988. This means the average "investment" was bought and sold three and one-half times during each year and was therefore held for less than four months. It doesn't take much imagination to see how long-term investors could actually pay more in internal trading commissions in this no-load fund than they would have paid in the loaded Pioneer Fund, which held stocks an average of six years during this same period.

And commissions are only one expense to consider when trading. The difference between the buy and sell prices of stocks is incredibly important but seldom analyzed by those who debate costs of owning a fund. Some very respected studies have shown these costs, combined with commission costs, can be as high as 4% for an average buy and sell executed by the fund.

If you doubt that, consider that if you buy a stock with a 9 3/4 bid (the selling price in the marketplace) and a $10 ask (the buying price in the marketplace), the 1/4 difference is 2.5% of your investment! A large buy for a fund could easily push the purchase price to $10 1/8 and a large sell could easily push the sell price to 9 5/8—and the 1/2 difference would be 5%! And we haven't even discussed commission costs yet! Even if you conservatively assume the costs are one-half of that, a 2% cost of buying and selling three and one-half times each year means these costs alone would be 7% EACH YEAR. It's hard for me to see how that's an inexpensive means of owning an investment.

I also believe there are costs to our society for this type of trading. *Newsweek* recently featured an article about why the Japanese continue to buy American companies and land. In a section suggesting that we "get our own act together" it stated: "In Japan, large corporations can rely on 'patient capital': long-term institutional investors keep their money in big companies almost no matter what happens to earnings in a given quarter. That permits major Japanese firms to make huge investments in R & D [research and development of new products and technology], plant and equipment without getting penalized by the markets."[2]

It's no secret that American companies are often pressured by investors' preoccupation with short-term performance. The Deloitte and Touche survey of ethics in America notes: "The pressure for short-term earnings was viewed by all respondents as the second greatest threat to ethics, just slightly behind the threat posed by decay in cultural and social institutions."

The Wall Street Journal added to the consensus on 18 October 1989 by stating: "Some people think the search for liquidity is fruitless. In 1936, John Maynard Keynes wrote that 'of all the maxims of orthodox finance none, surely, is more anti-social than the fetish of liquidity.' It leads investors to focus on short-term price movements—'a game of musical chairs,' he called it—rather than on long-term fundamental valuation."

It is my opinion that those mutual fund traders who day by day (or even hour by hour) switched money, joined with options players, financial futures players, and large-but-shortsighted pension funds to kill the market in October 1987. Ironically, the loss of confidence in our public markets from that episode has been harmful not only to industry and investment firms but also to many mutual fund companies. These players should be mindful of the old adage "live by the sword, die by the sword" as they promote the ability to get in and out quickly as some sort of marketing panacea. And the Christian investor should ask, "Does God really want me to add to that kind of fear and turmoil for our society?"

2 "Japan Goes Hollywood," *Newsweek* (9 October 1989): 72.

Christian investors need to seriously analyze whether their mutual funds, pension funds, or personal accounts are engaged in pursuing quick profits that may be not only an expensive hindrance to their performance but also very costly to our society's long-term prosperity.

There are three other basic points we need to consider about mutual funds. For example, this is how the *Individual Investor's Guide* describes the Fidelity Value Fund's objectives: "Seeks capital growth through investment in securities of companies that possess valuable fixed assets, or securities that fund management believes to be undervalued in the marketplace because of changes in the company, the economy, or the industry." The prospectus of the fund reads much the same way. These are truly remarkable goals when "investing" for four-month periods!

Second, the fund does have a decent track record, and I would recommend it to your attention if your only interest is the returns it has posted over the years. I would also add that Fidelity is a superb company and operates some funds I would recommend to your attention. But if you aren't sure that short-term trading adds to the stability of our world or creates jobs by employing capital efficiently, I would guide you to another fund.

Finally, you should notice that holding a stock for six years before taking a profit is a form of tax-deferral. Trading every four months guarantees you'll pay taxes each year on any profits you make, which is not viewed as optimal tax management.

Separate "style" from "substance" by looking beneath the surface of mutual funds. Any mutual fund prospectus will contain charts showing two expenses not discussed in the load versus no-load debate. "Operating Expenses" are figured for you and "Portfolio Turnover

189

Rate" allows you to estimate the additional internal costs of trading paid by your fund. I personally hesitate when funds show operating expenses above 1% annually and portfolio turnovers in excess of 50% each year. I prefer much lower figures in both categories.

I should point out that some no-load funds do invest for the long run and some load funds do trade (the worst of all possible worlds). I have used this example to point out that things aren't always what they seem in investment promotions, media analysis, and even independent advice. YOU need to look closely at the costs to you and your neighbor when investing your money.

It is also true that the average load fund has not outperformed the average no-load fund. But I've been in this business for over a decade and have yet to have someone ask for an "average" fund. They always seem to want the "best" funds. For example, one of the best shopping lists of funds for a longer-term investor is the "Honor Roll" of funds published by *Forbes* magazine each year. I analyzed this list last year and wrote the following to *Forbes*, since I have always felt they maintain an editorial bias toward no-load funds. It was published in their 17 October 1988 issue: "There are 19 funds in this year's Honor Roll; 4 are no-load and 15 impose a load of one nature or another. According to your figures, a $10,000 investment in each of the 4 no-loads would have accumulated an average of $50,806 per fund. A $10,000 investment in the other 15 would have accumulated an average of $61,583 per fund, after paying the sales charge!"

In 1989, 12 funds dropped off the list and 13 were added. Of the 20 funds in 1989's Honor Roll, 4 are no-load and 16 have some sort of load. The question of "What do I do with the 12 funds that dropped off?" is unanswered to this point. If you can answer such questions, I suggest you buy the no-load funds listed. If you

can't, I suggest you seek a competent broker or financial planner.

A portfolio manager is probably the single most important factor in choosing a mutual fund.

I believe the best way to pick a fund is to find the
most astute manager with an investing style you're comfortable with and keep the money in his or her hands
over a long period of time. You will need to look at both
loads and no-loads if you want to do that, since some of
the best managers work for both types. Use no-load
funds for short-term money and choose the best all-
around fund possible for longer-term money. And as
you read the volumes of debate about costs, remember
this solitary line from the 3 August 1989 *The Wall Street
Journal*: "A portfolio manager is probably the single
most important factor in choosing a mutual fund."

The most widespread problem for mutual fund investors is that most advertising, media listings, and advisers do not consider risk when they suggest different
funds. Most simply rank the returns the funds have
generated (usually over a short period of time) and
therefore are actually pointing out funds that took large
risks to make large returns.

One of the best ways to avoid this is to examine
Morningstar's Mutual Fund Values Report (the address
for this service is in the resource center at the end of
the book), which pays particular attention to the risk
side of the risk-reward equation.

Understanding Morningstar's Mutual Fund Values Report

I like to check the following eight items—at a minimum—before buying any fund:

❶ This section says American Mutual (our example here) offers "Above Average" returns with "Low" risk and therefore merits five stars (*****), their highest ranking.

❷ The maximum sales charge. Lower sales charges are available for larger purchases.

❸ The current income generated by the fund.

❹ The 3, 5, and 10 year "total return" averages. Total return is income plus growth. This example shows average annual total returns of 13.87%, 17.91% and 18.09% for the respective periods.

❺ Risk-return analysis. Numbers are relative to 1.00, the average fund's number. The 1.12 under "return" means this fund has done 12% better than the average fund. The .63 under "risk" means it has done that with 37% less risk than the average fund.

❻ The analyst's discussion. I do not tend to be "contrarian" of these particular recommendations since they are long-term in view and consider risk very thoroughly. Since many of the best funds are "contrarian" in nature, you'll be with the crowd if you go "contrarian" to the "contrarians"!

❼ The manager's name and the year he started managing the fund. The "et. al." means American Mutual employs a multiple manager system (several managers for the one fund).

❽ A listing of the fund's largest holdings.

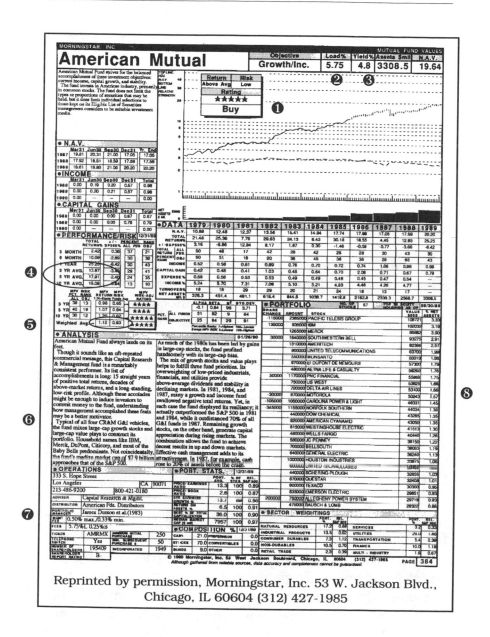

Reprinted by permission, Morningstar, Inc. 53 W. Jackson Blvd., Chicago, IL 60604 (312) 427-1985

Morningstar also provides a review of the annual portfolio turnovers at the bottom of the page, which I believe is an important consideration. They often, but not always, provide data that indicates whether the fund uses social screens of some nature.

Money Management

Another way to participate in the market is personalized money management, using a "money manager." This is appealing to those who want a custom portfolio and more responsiveness from the manager. (See chapter 10, "Choosing Investment Counsel," for more information.)

Media Management

Be careful when using the media for suggestions about stocks and funds. Advertisements and listings about last year's best fund or best stock is like buying clothes marked "30% to 40% MORE." The press has a lot of good uses, but listing investments on a daily, weekly, quarterly, or annual basis is not one of them—at least for most conservative investors.

As *The Wall Street Journal* said on 6 April 1989: "The flip-flop highlights an uncanny pattern in funds' quarterly performance. In the past several years, one quarter's champ is often the next quarter's chump." But they still publish them.

I really see very little value in these listings. You certainly shouldn't buy from them. And you know your fund is up if you already own it. Thus, they would only seem to be of interest to traders. The media usually discourages investors from taking suggestions about trading monthly or quarterly from investment firms. I only wish the media knew how many investors are encouraged to move around by following their lists and ads.

It's also interesting to note that had you simply bought the "top ten" performing funds each year during the 1980s, you would *never* have bought the Fidelity Magellan Fund, which was the top performing fund of the decade. Steady performance—not one-year hot streaks—wins investment races.[3]

Investing Versus Trading and Gambling

You wouldn't think of buying a Chevron service station today and selling it next week. Your Chevron stock deserves the same consideration.

You may find counselors who think you should trade Chevron or other stocks around for "bigger returns." I suggest you go along only IF they can provide you with proof (a proven track record) that it works. You can do this by asking for the counselor's tax return for the past two years.

Sounds tough? Not really. Most investment planners ask for your tax returns. And you'd ask for the same if you were deciding whether to buy a business. Essentially, these counselors are asking you to enter the trading business, and they either have a track record or they don't. Compare the record to a mutual fund managed by some of the people mentioned in this book and make your own decisions. Be sure to include intangibles such as stress, risk, and allocated time.

Many brokers, planners, and journalists who encourage trading really think they can make money for you (I did myself for quite a while). There is a national contest called the U.S. Trading and Investing Championships. It's been in existence for about five years, and brokers and investors from across the country pay a couple of hundred dollars to enter it.

These self-proclaimed trading experts do not enter just to create commissions from their own accounts or sell you on a market timing letter. They really think

---

3 *The Wall Street Journal* (13 March 1990): C-1.

they can make money. Yet *The Wall Street Journal* recently reported that only 23% of these experts had made money during this period of generally rising stock prices. True, there were some who had made incredible returns during this period, but it's doubtful that they'll be the ones calling you at dinnertime trying to get your business.

Pure Speculation

Many people today are interested in "options" on stocks and "futures" on the stock market. These are a highly leveraged means of betting on the future direction of a stock or bond. An important point to note here is that in these transactions you don't actually own stocks or bonds; you just bet on their direction. My experience is that these make no sense from a practical point of view and cannot make sense from an ethical point of view—which leads to a discussion of the difference between "investing" and "gambling."

A gambling casino works on the principle that for every dollar someone makes, there is someone losing an equal amount (plus whatever the casino charges). But that is not true with investments such as stocks and real estate because investments do not have a particular time (such as the end of the card game) when there are winners and losers.

For example, someone could have bought IBM at $10 per share in the 1930s, someone else could have bought it for $20 in the 1940s, and so forth. This can happen because, over the longer term, companies become more productive and the government increases the amount of money in circulation to accommodate our increases in population or for other reasons. Some of this additional money finds its way into investments and prevents someone from having to lose just so someone else can win.

Steady performance — not one-year hot streaks — wins investment races.

Unfortunately, options and futures do have a short-term period when winners and losers are declared. I personally have decided that Christian principles do not allow me to win if someone else has to lose. The major thesis of this book is to propose that we can truly prosper while others do the same . . . *if we operate by certain standards.* I see nothing of that in options and futures as they're typically used.

Most people who trade commodities and options seem to feel they are simply competing against others who sit in brokerage offices across the country. In reality, they often compete with professionals in the pits, large companies and syndications armed with tens of millions of dollars, computers, and very expert personnel who do nothing but trade the markets. You have to be a "cockeyed optimist" to believe you can prevail over these odds in the long run.

These "investments" are sold in two ways: as "speculations" (which many Christians avoid) and as "portfolio insurance" (which many Christians buy, thinking it is prudent). With the latter, you are essentially purchasing these vehicles to protect you against market declines. It sounds a little like term insurance and is often sold that way. However, in principle there is a difference. When you buy term insurance, the company invests your premium over the years and no one has to lose when you make a claim. With "portfolio insurance," however, the money is not invested but simply transferred from a loser to a winner (minus fees of course). This has to bc an ethical problem for those who believe that we should "do unto others . . . ."

I buy insurance on my life because history has demonstrated that young men can and do die and affect the lives of their loved ones. I have seen no similar evidence that a conservative, balanced portfolio will die and affect the lives of its owners. In fact, history has proven that markets tend to go higher rather than die. Markets do become sick from time to time, but I do not invest money in a way that cannot withstand these relatively short periods (which is what portfolio insurance covers).

I've also noticed this form of insurance tends to be bought AFTER periods like October 1987, which is after-the-fact and therefore of questionable merit. And be assured, many very large investors were sold on the merits of this "insurance" before the crash, only to harshly discover that it didn't work.

It's possible that the original intent of these financial instruments—that is, of allowing institutional money to flow easily into and out of the markets—may have had some degree of legitimacy. But it's difficult to believe that all the speculative activity in futures and options will benefit our society in financing our future.

John Train, respected money manager and author, recently wrote: "Lynch [Peter Lynch of the Magellan Fund] deplores the absorption by the options market of the funds that once went into the shares of smaller companies. The option market is a gigantic, useless, expensive gambling casino, whereas the same money might have been available to finance small, new companies which really need it."[4]

---

4 John Train, *The New Money Masters* (New York: Harper and Row, 1989), 223.

Each Wall Street investment firm needs to seriously study whether they're jeopardizing the future well-being of our children with this financial form of instant gratification. And these firms are not the only ones. Recently *The Wall Street Journal* noted that three of the top "index arbitragers" on the Street (the widely criticized practitioners who use options and futures for short-term gains in the market) were the money management arms of three of our largest banking institutions.[5] So answers need to come from several places.

But were less money flowing into this senseless speculation, more money might be flowing to our small growth companies. Then these companies wouldn't need to issue junk bonds. Then investors might buy more Treasury bonds and Ginnie Maes. And then we might house our people and stop our foreign borrowing. Something to think about.

Modern Americans have created many ways to benefit at our neighbor's expense. But lest you become too cynical about our age, you should note that back in his day John Calvin "bitterly opposed the buying of interest without security, avaricious speculation, and the accumulation of wealth at the expense of one's neighbors." He obviously didn't deal with our modern versions of these abuses in the forms of junk bonds and credit card lending, options and futures speculation, or the governmental transfers of insurance and tax dollars from some people to others; but he did face other forms of the same problems back several hundred years ago.

Christian investors must try to employ their money in forms that will produce something positive for their neighbors, who will gladly prosper them in return. Cer-

---

5 "Institutions Remain Big Program Traders Amid Uproar," *The Wall Street Journal* (30 October 1989): C-1.

tainly the chance of reciprocation is infinitely greater than if we use our money in ways that either do nothing for our neighbors or actually harm them. It's only logical that speculators are doing everything possible to assure they don't prosper you (or actually do worse to you). But if we own companies that produce needed goods and services, people will gladly give to us in return. This might be viewed as a modern sub-theme of "seek first the kingdom of heaven and all this will be added unto you." It's only logical if you seriously think about it.

The Long-Term View

Buying stock in unpopular, high-quality companies that provide valuable goods and services and holding on for years does two things. First, it reduces risk because most of these are down in price due to their unpopularity. Second, we won't be tempted to sell them when they bounce up 15% or 20% in price. Phrases such as "you can't go wrong taking a profit" or "a bird in the hand" will not prevent us from having the large gains so essential to investing success.

Treat your stock like an investment, not like a gambling chip.

One of the very few investors who has experienced the success of John Templeton and Peter Lynch is the legendary Warren Buffet. Recently he described his approach to investing:

> Our new investments are not based on a judgment about short-term prospects for the stock market.

Rather, they reflect an opinion about long-term business prospects for specific companies. We do not have, never have had, and never will have an opinion about where the stock market, interest rates, or business activity will be a year from now. When we own portions of outstanding businesses with outstanding management, our favourite holding period is forever.[6]

I understand that's a bit extreme for most of us. But at least stick with your stocks until there is clearly a better value for the money. Most investors have better luck with their small businesses and homes because they treat them as investments; but they treat their stocks like poker chips. Don't follow that practice or allow others to do it on your behalf.

Ethical Questions

The Calvert Group offers an ethical mutual fund, and their investment guidelines, as discussed in their sales brochure, are also good guidelines for the Christian investor:

> The Fund's founders examined the issues most of us are concerned about. War. Peace. Oppression. Human dignity. The environment. The workplace. . . . The Fund seeks to invest in companies that support their workers, provide opportunities for women and minorities, and deliver safe products and services in ways that sustain our natural environment. The Fund will not invest in oppressive regimes such as South Africa, the manufacture of weapons systems or the production of nuclear energy.

Similar funds, such as the Pax World Fund, Parnassus Fund, and others listed in the resource center, do more stringent screening than the traditional "sin

---

6 "Capitalism Survey," *The Economist* (5 May 1990): 15.

stock" screening of alcohol, tobacco, and gambling that has been the case for some in the past. And there are professional money managers who do a similar type of screening for those with larger amounts to invest. Most will allow you to develop your own criteria for investing so you can tailor a portfolio that meets both your needs and your ethical standards. I particularly recommend these managers to church pension funds, seminaries, and similar groups.

You probably can't apply quite as stringent screening to your portfolio of individual stocks, but you can do a reasonable job by paying attention to the businesses they are in, by reading annual reports, by asking questions of management, and by evaluating Wall Street research reports. You might also want to subscribe to one of the newsletters listed in the resource center if you are fairly active and interested.

Utility stock investors might want to reflect on the merits of nuclear power when evaluating their portfolios. Personally I am undecided about whether nuclear power is necessary to our future or not, but anything that causes picket lines and protests will have trouble with regulators over the years. And increased regulation is usually a drag on earnings. Nuclear power plants have also been expensive propositions. So I have decided to avoid them on practical grounds. There are plenty of other utilities to invest in until the question marks are erased. (The "Business" section of a Value Line report tells of any nuclear power activities.)

I subscribe to a newsletter about socially responsible investments called *Good Money* which maintains its own utility index of basically non-nuclear utilities. This index has outperformed the Dow Jones Utility Index by 198.7% to 66% from 1976 to September 1988. Whether you agree with nuclear power or not, it seems that investing in a way that seeks to avoid possible harm to humanity has proven rewarding.

Environmental Ethics

In Leviticus 25:3–4 we read these words: "You shall plant your fields, prune your vineyards, and gather your crops for six years. But the seventh year is to be a year of complete rest for the land, a year dedicated to the LORD." In giving this admonition through Moses, God was saying that the earth is not just here for our convenience. We have to respect it and care for it if we want to reap its benefits. Caring for God's creation is an act of worship.

The Reverend R. T. Brooks provides a commentary appropriate for our day when he writes:

> It was a momentous day indeed when man became strong enough to inflict a mortal wound on his environment and to upset the balance of nature on this planet irrevocably. And this momentous day fell in our time. Plenty of local damage had been done before, but people now young are the first ever to be born into an age when they could make this earth incapable of sustaining human life. The tender sense of unity with and responsibility for the creation is both biblical and necessary.[7]

On the very first day of the new decade, 1990, in his message released for World Day of Peace, Pope John Paul II said:

> Today the ecological crisis has assumed such proportions as to be the responsibility of everyone. Christians, in particular, realize their responsibility within creation and their duty toward nature and the Creator are an essential part of their future.

---

7 R. T. Brooks, *Ask the Bible* (Gramercy Publishing, 1989), 96.

The Reverend J. Andy Smith III, who directs Social and Ethical Responsibility in Investments for the National Ministries of the American Baptist Churches, recently prepared a brief for the Interfaith Center on Corporate Responsibility about a broad environmental movement developed for corporations. Called the "Valdez Principles," it encourages environmental awareness for the business community. He writes:

> On September 7, 1989, a coalition of pension funds, church groups, environmental organizations and social investment analysts launched a new program to defend the environment—the Valdez Principles. Named for the tragic Exxon tanker Valdez, the Principles set forth ten goals for corporate behavior. They call on corporations to measure their profits only after adding up *all* costs of business.

That it might be in the best interests of shareholders and company executives alike to closely monitor the activities that cause pollution is clearly reflected in a 15 May 1989 *Forbes* article that discussed the toxic waste dumps around the country.

> The estimated cost of cleaning up the nation's 10,000-plus toxic waste dumps: a staggering $500 billion over the next 50 years. . . . Sums like that could easily put into Chapter 11 (bankruptcy) some thinly capitalized or overleveraged companies.

Even some blue-chip companies will experience a significant decline in earnings when they have to spend enormous amounts to eliminate their messes from our landscape. Having screened out companies that create these environmental dangers on a day-to-day basis, ethical investors will have a decided advantage in their returns.

To do this, you will probably need to subscribe to a newsletter or use a mutual fund that monitors such activities. Annual reports do not usually discuss a company's pollution problems. Some of the funds and managers look for companies that actually clean the environment, some seek companies that do not pollute to begin with, and some use a mixture of the two. (See listing in the resource center.)

While I urge you to make environmental factors a part of your investing universe, I would also urge you to play a part on a more individual level. As *Forbes* recently noted: "We must shed the easy belief that pollution is caused solely by corporate greed. It is not. It is caused by us, all of us, because we want convenient products and we want them cheap." This statement ignores factors such as researching, developing, and marketing products that pollute, but there is a very valid point here.

International Investing

International investing is a major trend that promises to explode during the 1990s and beyond. The U.S. stock market comprised about two-thirds of the world's market in 1970; today it is a little over one-third. The numbers are similar for the world's bond markets.

From a growth perspective, the various world markets have shown as much potential as ours. In fact, only once in the last ten years (1982) was the U.S. stock market the best performer in the world, and there have been years when the U.S. market declined while most others rose. For that reason alone, several studies indicate that global diversification can add stability to your portfolio.

Some of my clients have a "one world" approach to investing, while others view international investing as "un-American." I have found no biblical principles that promote nationalism and discourage international investing, but the author of Proverbs and Ecclesiastes does differentiate between borrowing from "foreigners" and "investing in foreign trade." An important consideration today.

Global Investing recently quoted John Templeton, considered the dean of global investing, as saying:

> Global investing has enormous advantages from a standpoint of knowledge of other people. By making us more knowledgeable about other countries it promotes understanding of other people around the world. Worldwide brotherhood is promoted by it. . . . The more worldwide investing there is, the better off from a spiritual standpoint, peace, brotherhood, and especially prosperity. If you have world trade where each nation produces what it's best in, then the commercial interaction of nations will work for everyone. The growth of prosperity in the world will be greater when we can all invest in each other's progress. That's a very inspiring idea for me.

I personally believe that the increasing ability to move money across national boundaries will help assure a higher level of integrity on the part of political and business leaders. Money will flee a nation that insists on the destruction of its money. Shareholders will naturally gravitate to well-managed companies that produce products of integrity in responsible ways. Rapid changes can bring problems, of course, but the overall effect could be very positive in the long run.

Be aware that there are pitfalls in diversifying your investing on an international scale. Avoid a do-it-your-self approach and consider a good mutual fund. Some of the fund groups listed in the resource center offer international investments.

Growth with Income

I would like to make one final, but critical suggestion about the stock market. Over the years I have noticed that my retired clients tend to move more and more money to guaranteed, interest-bearing investments, and I encourage that to a point. But many seem to be doing that very heavily while inflation continues and they are living longer and longer. In other words, even they need some of the growth that is typically offered by stocks in order to keep up. Therefore, I suggest they explore a "systematic withdrawal" plan from a conservative mutual fund that has a proven track record.

Most mutual funds can send you a monthly check at a specified rate, regardless of what the fund is earning. Some years the fund will not earn what you withdraw and you'll dip into principal. But in other years the fund will earn more than you are withdrawing and thus will continue to grow in value. Historically, many funds have provided excellent income while growing in value. You can ask your broker or no-load fund for a computer illustration. I would suggest you examine one for 5, 10, and 15 year periods.

The fact that there is no guarantee that you'll earn what you'll withdraw bothers some people. But over the years I've learned there are few things guaranteed in life. Some of my clients who stayed in money market investments during the 1980s have either reduced their standard of living or invaded their principal as their incomes dropped due to falling interest rates. There is little guarantee in that. During the same period, the better mutual funds performed beautifully with the systematic withdrawal approach. So one investment approach offsets the other. That's the beauty of a diversified investment plan and makes it worth your examination.

Summary

I've seen a lot of investments come and go during my years on Wall Street. High quality stocks of well-managed companies continue to be a top choice of pension fund managers, trust companies, insurance companies, and other knowledgeable investors. And I believe the Christian investor should consider owning stock in those businesses engaged in productive, ethical endeavors. Clean products and clean profits can create real wealth for our families, our country, and our world.

Many Christians seem to feel that investing in the stock market is simply another form of gambling. Perhaps they would have a different understanding if they would view stock as what it really is: part of the ownership of a business. And if investors would view stock as ownership, rather than as gambling chips, they would buy, manage, and sell much more wisely and responsibly. In return, their "business" will treat them well "one of these days."

9

Economics of Real Estate Investing

Good people make good institutions

James W. Frick

MOST AMERICANS KNOW THAT real estate has been a profitable investment over the years, but few fully understand why. And even those who do often don't realize that some of the reasons have changed in recent years, greatly affecting the nature of real estate investing. Surprisingly, many of these changes make the teachings of the Mosaic Law regarding the land more relevant than ever. The long and the short of this means that it is important to study the usefulness and economic merits of real estate and not rely solely on the future appreciation of property.

Special or Speculative?

Real estate is a very difficult subject to discuss in a general way because it is so "local" in nature. In the mid-1980s, for example, real estate was booming in New England and collapsing in Texas. By the late 1980s it was collapsing in New England but beginning to recover in Texas. As real estate professionals say, "Location, location, location."

Real estate has always been a hedge against inflation. Buildings tend to go up in value as wood, bricks, and labor go up in price. Because they believe inflation is a fact of life, many investors buy real estate. While this may be true, there are other influences on real estate that you need to seriously explore.

For example, over the years real estate has been the beneficiary of favorable governmental policies. The government has always been interested in encouraging the ownership of real estate, so they have continued to legislate certain benefits for its development and ownership. Depreciation is one such benefit. Depreciation allows you to take a tax deduction each year (pretend the value has gone down), even if the value of your real es-

211

tate goes up. Stocks and bonds could hardly compete with that over the years.

The government used to let you have part of your gain tax-free via a favorable capital-gains tax. This looked real good when compared to the full tax you paid on government bonds and CDs. Small wonder many investors compared and bought real estate.

Lastly, government policies have made very favorable, fixed-rate loans available to buy real estate, and the federal insurance offered by the savings and loan industry assured money would be available for real estate financing. Those who financed real estate investments with 10% down and a fixed 6% interest rate would have put a lot more down and paid a lot more interest if they had wanted to finance the purchase of stocks instead. However, real estate generally hasn't appreciated any faster than most quality stocks over the years. So, the real secret of real estate was in the financing.

The real secret of real estate was in the financing.

A house bought for $20,000 in 1955 and worth $200,000 today probably isn't ten times as useful for the people living there. The house can sell for more because of inflation, our attitudes about our homes, and because of the government's well-intentioned incentives that have encouraged the ownership of real estate for the past few decades. These factors escalated the price of real estate, making it too expensive for many people to own. Concern that housing was becoming unaffordable was a factor in Congress's reducing some of these incentives. The appreciation of real estate and the recently changed incentives have created a very new environment.

Prices are obviously higher, which in turn increases the risk. This seems obvious, but I'm amazed how many people ignore this simple fact. (Indeed, it often seems that investors fall more and more in love with investments as they get more and more expensive.) Inflation hasn't disappeared, but it has slowed. Fixed-rate mortgages are expensive, if available at all for investment properties. Depreciation allowances have been reduced in value. And there is no more capital-gains tax advantage. All these items make it crucial to watch the true economics of real estate. We can't just count on inflation to bail us out of mistakes in the future.

The good news for the ethical investor is that these recent changes should tend to reduce speculation in the real estate sector, which in turn will slow the price spiral that has denied affordable housing to so many of our younger families and the disadvantaged.

You can buy properties on your own if you have the time, money, and expertise. This is your most productive option—if you know what you are doing. Otherwise, you should consider the following options.

Partnerships

One very popular option is the real estate partnership. I classify partnerships much like I classify stocks: speculative, growth, and income.

How the Real Estate Picture Has Changed

1. Fixed-rate mortgages are expensive, if available at all.

2. Depreciation allowances have been reduced in value.

3. No more capital-gains tax advantage.

You can speculate by buying property and hoping someone will want to put an office building or a shopping center on it. You can also speculate by buying property with a-less-than-loyal group of renters, hoping the rental situation improves or that inflation rises. Both of these require gambling on the future, which I'm not willing to do.

Growth properties possess more stable rental bases, but they are financed fairly heavily to magnify any gains on the value of the property. I avoid virtually all of these because of the risks of the borrowing. Suppose you put down $20,000 on a $100,000 property. If the property appreciates to $120,000, you've made $20,000 on a $20,000 investment. If the property depreciates to $80,000, however, you have lost all your money. I tend to avoid "double or nothing" investments these days.

I do look at income properties, such as occupied apartment buildings, office buildings, or shopping centers. I'll consider properties with mortgages up to about 50% of the property's value. Here the income is relatively predictable but not fixed because tenants can come and go as leases expire. Inflation should add some value to the properties over the years, and income is tax advantaged since some depreciation benefits remain. Modest income, modest appreciation, and modest tax advantages can add up to solid returns.

The Most Conservative Real Estate?

"Net lease" income properties have been good to my clients over the years. An example is the easiest way to explain this. TECO is the electric company in the Tampa, Florida, area. A few years ago TECO decided to sell its corporate headquarters but didn't want to move. My firm put an investor group together to buy it, and TECO signed a long-term lease. TECO gets to stay in their home and invest their proceeds in power plants or whatever; the investor group gets a dependable renter. In this type of arrangement the renter can re-buy the property, at a fair price, several years in the future. This is also done with bank buildings, corporate buildings, and motels.

Betting on the future makes little sense. Borrowing heavily to bet on the future makes even less sense.

Properly done, net lease real estate can be a good arrangement for the conservative investor. Most of these properties pay more income than others because the appreciation ·potential is less. The risk of vacancies is reduced if you choose the tenants properly, and you know there is an economic need for the properties because they are usually occupied when you buy them. Inflation risk is reduced because the leases are written to increase your income if inflation worsens. And damages from the failure of a renter are reduced since you still own the building if the corporation breaks the lease. However, the financial condition of your renter is a critical consideration in this transaction.

Net lease properties are not get-rich-quick properties. My clients bought them in the early 1980s with expectations of an 8% income that would increase with inflation. Other partnerships, which counted on high inflation and heavy borrowing, were showing track records of 20%, 30%, and even 40% after the inflationary 1970s. *The Wall Street Journal* did a study of how several of these partnerships are doing and published the results in November 1988. Many of the partner-

215

ships which essentially bet on high inflation continuing were down from 40% to 60% in price. None of the partnerships studied were being bought at higher prices than investors originally paid—except one. That was the net lease partnership. It was being bought at 20% higher prices since moderate inflation had increased its income substantially.

Real estate is simply another area where betting on the future makes little sense. Borrowing heavily to bet on it makes even less sense. Basing value on usefulness is a much better gauge of real economic merit. Any investment that provides a steady stream of increasing income is always going to be valuable. This may be the closest thing to a modern equivalent of the Mosaic plot of land that produced crops year after year (assuming you can't own a farm).

Basics of Limited Partnerships

A limited partnership is simply a large pool of money from hundreds of investors assembled by a manager or an investment firm. This money is invested in large properties by the partnership manager. This means that you do nothing except contribute the money (usually a $5,000 minimum) so it is very convenient. Naturally this convenience has its price. Real estate has never been inexpensive to own in any form. Hiring others to select, buy, finance, manage, and sell properties is even more expensive. In the past people paid little attention to such costs because they made so much money despite them. These days, however, investors are taking a closer look.

Controlling Costs

You need to be a Philadelphia lawyer to understand the costs in partnerships because of the number of dif-

216

ferent types of fees that can be involved. The salesperson's commission is typically 7% to 8%. Then there are acquisition fees, management fees, and incentive fees if the properties are sold at a profit. Some partnerships from brokers and planners claim to be "no-load." A strong word of caution here: Be skeptical of anyone going to the trouble of selecting and managing real estate for you simply because they like you.

There is a widely quoted service called "The Stanger Ratings" that analyzes fees in the more popular partnerships. These analysts look at all the fees in a partnership and assign ratings ranging from AAA+ down. Important note: These are not safety ratings. They simply analyze how fair the fee structures are. I would stick with programs rated AA and up. The Standard and Poor's organization issues a "Current Partnership Offering Report" that analyzes fees and other items for a smaller number of partnerships.

It is not easy to get your money out of a partnership if you want it back, especially if you want it back in a hurry. It's not a lot different from owning a house you need to sell. You may have to sell at a bargain price if you want to sell quickly. I sometimes buy distress sales (fairly, I hope) for my clients from other brokers at reasonable discounts. Believe me, most real estate is not the place to invest money you may want to liquidate in a hurry, and partnerships are seldom exceptions.

There *are* ways to go wrong when buying limited partnerships. I was recently offered one, owned by a client of another broker, that had an AAA rating when issued about a year ago. I could have bought it at 80 cents on the dollar, and it would have paid over 10% at that price. The partnership had purchased the properties for cash and the properties had very high occupancy levels. But I turned it down.

Why? Because there are some creative ways to make income partnerships look better than they really are. For example, a partnership may finance the up-front fees of organizing and selling the partnership with mortgages that do not require periodic interest payments (called zero-coupon mortgages), which allows all your money to be invested in real estate and prevents monthly interest payments that reduce your net income. This allows the partnership to generate more "income." Unfortunately, the mortgages get bigger and bigger as the interest accumulates and must be paid off eventually. The bill for the free lunch will definitely arrive.

Some partnerships also "defer" the fees for managing the real estate for a while. This inflates your income for a couple of years— but once again, the bill will arrive.

Properties bought for cash pay about 4% or 5% at the time of this writing. Some partnerships pay 6% to 8% income. They may do this through "developer guarantees."

Suppose you had a rented house you wanted to sell me for $100,000. The rent is $5,000 a year, which is 5%. I'd like to get 8% or $8,000. I could pay you $106,000 for the house with you "guaranteeing" me $3,000 per year for the next two years in addition to my $5,000 rent. I now have $8,000 income per year and feel good— for about two years. Unfortunately, at this point my income declines to $5,000 and my $106,000 house is worth $100,000. Once again the bill arrives for my free lunch. And I may have passed up a better meal in the meantime.

There are some partnership promoters who argue that no one is hurt by these techniques because the added income makes up for any losses. I disagree. I believe many people buy these believing they can depend on the high income, which may not be there in a couple of years. They ignore bonds and other appropriate investments because they prefer their income with appreciation potential when possible. I'm a strong believer in the modest income and appreciation potential offered by most real estate, but to turn that into high income through free-lunch-financing gimmicks invites problems. Ignore any partnership using these techniques, and understand that partnership organizers don't go out of their way to explain these techniques to salespeople. Explore any prospectus thoroughly and get as many independent evaluations as possible.

A Little Extra Skepticism

"Partnerships are ventures that begin with the investors having the money and the managers having the experience. They end with the investors having the experience and the managers having the money."

That's an old joke in the business, but I'm afraid it is closer to the truth than most care to admit. There are some fine professional people in the partnership business today and they often get tarred with the same brush. But the reality remains that pooling tens of millions of dollars and describing the intentions of the organizer in a very thick prospectus was more temptation than many people could resist during the aggressive 1980s. If it's true that cynicism is the difference between promise and performance, some of these offerings did more than their share to create today's environment.

I personally expect the current problems in the industry to be addressed by the survivors, but I also suggest that in the meantime you exercise diligent care when investing. Get a prospectus on any partnership you are offered. It is complicated and therefore ignored by most people— and its sheer size can either inform you or conceal important information you need. Don't invest if you don't read. And it's critical that you pay particular attention to the people who will actually buy and manage your properties.

Other Avenues to Ownership

An approach to owning real estate that many seldom consider is through *insurance contracts.* Several variable annuities and variable life products have real estate options within the contracts. These seem to offer three primary advantages:

First, the costs seem very reasonable when compared to partnerships. Second, insurance companies have long track records in managing properties. They don't tend to jump in and out of the business. And third, real estate is normally a long-term, illiquid (not readily convertible into cash) investment. But that isn't so important when purchased with money intended for retirement or to be passed on to heirs, which is what insurance contracts encourage. And since there is now no long-term capital gains tax advantage for real estate, the tax-deferral that insurance contracts offer for income and gains from sales of property makes them compare favorably with alternatives such as partnerships. Should Congress reestablish a capital-gains tax, however, it would help partnerships again.

Another opportunity may be what is called a *real estate investment trust* (REITS). These are real estate holding companies that trade on a stock exchange just like other stocks. There are different types of REITS, but many simply own apartments and office buildings. These have a tendency to move in value opposite most stocks over the long run (high inflation is usually negative for stocks but good for these); therefore they can be an excellent diversification tool, offering a fairly stable income at attractive levels. You can find several REITS analyzed by Value Line and by major investment firms. Stay with high-quality and out-of-favor companies, as previously discussed. Avoid simply buying the ones paying the highest dividends. REITS are one way of buying a portfolio of diversified real estate for a few hundred dollars.

Another way is through a mutual fund. Several mutual fund groups offer funds that specifically invest in real estate and real estate-backed assets. Their primary attraction is that they can constantly look for different opportunities. This allows them to adjust to changing economic scenarios over the years. Some of these funds buy the common stocks of companies that own sizable real estate holdings. This can make sense during differing economic environments. The real estate values increase during periods of higher inflation, but the operating companies tend to do better during periods of slower inflation. That's a prudent approach.

Ethical Alternatives

The major ethical consideration in real estate is the screening of tenants. For example, I personally would rule out being landlord to a casino. A positive investment that would address one of our most pressing social needs might be partnerships that build and operate housing for lower-income families and the elderly. Often these offer special tax benefits to investors. I would like to make a blanket recommendation of any partnership that addresses this most critical area but often find syndication fees, sales fees, and debt are so high that I cannot do this. Many offerings simply change the ownership of properties rather than create additional housing. It will do little for the needy if too much of our investment goes to organizers, salespeople, banks, and previous owners. But the thoughtful Christian investor should seriously consider any partnerships that address this need and do it efficiently.

Few areas demand the Christian's attention as much as this one. According to the recent American Housing Survey, as reported in *The Wall Street Journal*, the number of poor households in the U.S. increased 19% between 1978 and 1985. The survey also found that the supply of housing the poor can even begin to afford shrank 19% in the same period. If you are laboring under the impression that all homeless are "boozers and misfits," you should review a study by the U.S. Conference of Mayors that found one in four homeless are employed and that families are the fastest growing segment of the homeless.

The same survey reports that the government spent $32 billion for low-income housing programs in 1979. In 1988 it spent less than $8 billion. Clearly the government is counting on President Bush's "thousand points of light" to create the glow from the windows of privately built and financed homes for the disadvantaged. There are a tremendous number of organizations working to fill the gap vacated by the government, but they are rapidly losing the battle. Christians would do well to answer the call for reinforcements in ways that do the most good for the money.

Of all the needs of our society that I've tried to address through the investment markets, affordable housing has been the toughest. Subsidized housing partnerships look good on the surface but often simply buy existing housing rather than develop additional housing. And some can actually hurt if managed so they increase in value down the road. This can make the housing that does exist more expensive to the renters.

222

It is the down payment, not the monthly payment, that denies many home ownership.

I believe the true long-term solution is to get as many people as possible into their own homes, rather than into rental units. The pride and stability of home ownership could accomplish as much socially as the roofs could as shelter. And this may not be quite as impossible as it seems at first glance. Logic insists that if most of our poor can make rental payments, they can make a reasonable mortgage payment. The problem, of course, is accumulating the down payment while trying to feed a family. It is the down payment, not the monthly payment, that denies so many home ownership.

The only solution to this problem I've found so far is what's often known as "community loan funds," which are just large pools of money started or contributed to by churches, foundations, and other concerned groups and individuals across the country. The managers of these funds can lend to the needy for many purposes, but most concentrate on housing because of the great need. (The resource center provides addresses where you can write for information about these loan funds.)

Suppose a person needs an $8,000 down payment for a $40,000 house. An analysis reveals that this person can make the monthly payments, so the loan fund assists with the $8,000, often encouraging what is called "sweat equity" in fixing the house up a bit. The borrower makes an additional small monthly payment to the loan fund. Interestingly, these funds experience a very small percentage of loss— a percentage most banks would envy. An example of what happens when you finance people's needs rather than wants.

Good things happen when you finance people's needs rather than their wants.

As an investor, you could make almost any size loan. You could set your interest rate and maturity—the more conservative the rate and the longer the loan, the better for the funds of course. Rates comparable to those paid on savings accounts are the norm, although many loans are made at no interest. The loans are not insured by the federal government so you do share some risk (some banks, such as the South Shore Bank in Chicago, operate both competitive-rate and low-rate programs that are insured), but because it is shared with other lenders and because the fund is managed by caring, hands-on people, the risk is reduced.

This is the type of investment I believe a Moses or a Luther or a Calvin would be most comfortable with today, and it fills a social need I believe Christ might care about too.

As Christian investors, we should understand that our good fortune in appreciated real estate can mean that others cannot afford the new higher prices. If blessing implies responsibility, one approach might be to lend to a loan fund some of the profits inflation has produced (and especially those gains doubly blessed by exemption from income taxes by our over-age-55 exclusion). Notice that I'm not advocating giving all profit away, just sharing the benefits of our blessing with those who desperately need them.

Conclusion

Any conventional real estate investment should be reviewed for excessive borrowing and speculating on the future. Most of us ignored those principles in the early 1980s as we mortgaged heavily and bet on inflation continuing. Virtually every tax shelter created in America depended on those two factors (and the government's continued incentives). Most didn't succeed, however, because what we'd bet on didn't materialize.

Others bet heavily that thousands would move from a dead Detroit to a booming oil belt and would need thousands of apartments. Another bad bet. Similar bets were made on Florida and New York City condominiums. More failures.

It's critical to understand that if you need to guess the rate of inflation, the level of interest rates, or the population shifts in order to make money, it's probably speculation and not investment. Why not keep both your principles and your common sense firmly grounded and simply invest where there's a demonstrated need and where the investment is structured for the best use of the money.

While times will always change, most of our needs remain very much the same—which is a good reason for occasionally looking to the past.

Do I hear Moses, Calvin, and Luther chuckling?

10

Choosing Investment Counsel

*From now on, any definition of a successful
life must include serving others.*

President George Bush, 1989

ONE SUBJECT THAT AROSE several times among Jesus' disciples was the matter of "greatness." Perhaps that is why Christ made a point of settling the question before he left this earth. One of the ways he made his point was by washing the feet of his disciples. "Whoever wants to become great among you must be a servant," he said.

The modern world has many ways of defining greatness, especially when it comes to financial concerns. Titles, prestigious buildings and offices, corporate images, and diplomas serve as testimonies that we should value a particular form of counsel. Others advise us to judge quality on the basis of size or cost, the largest investment firm, a boutique investment firm, the most expensive counsel, or the least expensive service.

My experience, however, is that no one has improved on the example Jesus—and eventually his faithful disciples—provided two thousand years ago. The greatest counselors are dedicated, talented, caring people who humbly serve others.[1]

Investment Firms and the Supermarket Mentality

Several executives of major investment firms have compared our business to "financial supermarkets" and that's a pretty good analogy. A few years ago you could buy only groceries at the supermarket; today you can buy everything from magazines to motor oil. A few years

---

[1] This was the hardest chapter for me to write. I have been a commission broker for years—and not always the humblest servant. This does not mean that I believe the commission-based system is the best possible approach. There are large problems inherent in this system. But I also believe there is considerable self-serving criticism of the system that may not be in your best interest either. I'll try to be as objective as possible, but weigh my background as you read.

ago you bought stocks and bonds at investment firms; today you can buy everything from CDs to airplanes.

Your local supermarkets carry staples such as meat, milk, and vegetables. They also stock junk food—potato chips, candy, and soft drinks. The next time you visit, notice how your supermarket is arranged. The meat and milk and produce are usually in the back. You have to walk past the junk food to get to them. That's because the mark-ups are greater in potato chips than in lettuce. You'll rarely see an advertisement for lettuce, but you'll frequently see come-ons for potato chips and soft drinks.

Investment firms operate in similar fashion. We still carry staples such as blue-chip stocks and government bonds, but we also handle options, commodities, and junk bonds. The mark-ups on our "junk" are high too. Notice the promotions you get from an investment firm; often they're not featuring the staples.

The middle of the grocery store is devoted to "packaged goods," such as canned soups, canned vegetables, and bakery goods. These convenience products are designed for those who are either too busy to cook or who lack culinary desire or talent. Since someone else had to go to the trouble to clean, dice, and mix the vegetables, we pay for this convenience. The mark-ups are good on these items, although not as good as on the junk food.

You'll find a lot of "packaged products" at investment firms too. Mutual funds, unit trusts, and limited partnerships provide the convenience of having someone else pick and manage the investments for you. These are good for the busy investor or those lacking the talent or knowledge to pick and manage their own investments. You pay for the convenience of course, and the mark-ups are good for the investment firms.

One problem with canned goods is that the vegetables inside don't always look like the picture on the outside. You will find the same problem with packaged investment products. There are more and more of these competing for your dollar, so the pictures get prettier and prettier, but the stuff inside stays about the same. And you still get what you pay for too.

Being a true gourmet, I enjoy Campbell's Chicken Noodle Soup. My wife can make superb noodle soup from scratch (I guess) but there's little reason for her to do it as long as Campbell's keeps doing a good job. I feel much the same way about some packaged investments. There are mutual funds, unit trusts, and a few limited partnerships that you can count on to deliver what you pay for. Because you can't always trust the picture on the outside of the package, it's important to stay with these proven "brand-name" products.

That's not easy in either market today. Poster "sale" signs point to promotional products and someone always seems to be introducing a "new and improved" product. I bite on those occasionally and almost always wish I'd stayed with the "old and proven."

Your grocer does not have to believe that potato chips are good for you in order to stock them in the store. He simply makes them available if you want to buy them. Likewise, investment firm executives may not believe it's healthy for you to trade options with the assistance of a newly trained broker, but they offer you the choice.

It's very important to understand the changes that have developed with the supermarket mentality. Many experienced investors remember when they relied heavily on the advice of their investment firm, assuming they were dealing with a high degree of professionalism in every area that would make sure they got a "well-balanced diet." I believe that relationship is changing to one where some "supermarket" firms simply display the goods and let you buy what you want—or what seems the most attractive. (We've seen how dangerous that can be.) Madison Avenue advertising agencies sometimes imply that brokers are "nutritionists" who will guide you around the store and tell you what is good for you. Often, however, you get to the store and the brokers simply walk you past everything, a guided tour, and let you make your own choices about whether to pick the healthy offerings or the junk. Worse are those who advertise the nutritionist image while overtly guiding you to the junk food.

It is vital that you tell your firm and broker in very clear terms that while others may want to browse through the junk food, you want to be guided to the "healthy choices" at the back of the store. It's equally vital that you actually buy the "good stuff" after you see it, rather than the pretty packaging that promises more.

Wholesalers often encourage grocers to display certain of their products. The same is true at investment firms. Many investments are represented by salespeople who are called wholesalers by our industry. Some carry very fine products, and brokers see these representatives about once a year, knowing they can call if they have a question or problem. Then there are those who seem to pop in your office about every two weeks.

In all the years I have been in this business, I have never met a government bond wholesaler. Why? Because there's no such creature. Some investments sell themselves, and government bonds are among those. Others, however, require legions of wholesalers who call brokers constantly in order to move the product. One of the major reasons young brokers get investors in trouble is that they simply sell what is sold to them.

And odds are good that no wholesaler's been trying to sell them on the benefits of government bonds.

You may also have noticed that your grocery store puts its own label on many products. The theory is, "Why pay Campbell's to make the soup if we can make our own and pocket the difference?" It's perfectly logical from the grocer's viewpoint. But I like the way Campbell's has perfected the product over the years. They know how to make chicken soup.

Investment firms, banks, and insurance companies are doing much the same thing. They figure, "Why sell someone else's mutual fund if we can create our own and pocket the management fees?" Perfectly logical. Unfortunately, they don't realize how much those "tried and true" money managers have learned about making money over the years. They often just aren't in the same league. And while some store-brand products are a bit less expensive than brand names, that's not usually the case in investment firms.

I like my grocer, but I'll let Campbell's make my soup. I suggest you love your broker but ask him for investments that have proven themselves over the years—whether they are store-brand or otherwise.

Naturally you are interested in investments that make money for you and not just fees for your counselor. It's not always easy for brokers to show you those. Sometimes counselors get compensated considerably more (as much as 50% more, even though the commission charge to you is the same) for guiding you to the store-brand product. If store-brand products are truly competitive with other products, I see little reason for the broker to have such incentives to offer the store brands. Because this often is the case, however, you need a truly professional broker.

Working with a Broker

The bull market of the 1980s created boundless opportunities for ambitious new brokers. Investment firms expanded, and even banks and insurance companies began training brokers. As a result, the financial world is filled with brokers, but good ones can still be hard to find.

New brokers are bright, energetic, and eager to help you make your fortune. And they can be dangerous. (Especially in today's investment supermarkets, expanded with more and more products.) In fact, I don't think there's anything quite as dangerous as a new broker who seriously wants to help you get very rich.

The simple fact is that a new broker has to make mistakes, perhaps more than many new professionals, as there is no multi-year training program available for brokers. (Rest assured that some investors in Florida who read this book will know how some early Christians felt when they heard Saint Paul preach for the first time!) Experienced brokers make mistakes too, but theirs are usually fewer and less severe. You can do new brokers a favor by letting them learn with your money. You can do yourself a favor by letting them learn with someone else's.

There's nothing quite as dangerous as a new broker who seriously wants to help you get very rich.

Of course there is no *guarantee* you'll be ahead with an experienced broker. Your odds are improved but not certain. The same is true when choosing a broker with a title. I've never yet seen a title awarded solely for making clients money. Good salespeople are recognized as quickly as good brokers. So if possible, you need to know a broker's heart and capabilities.

Referral is the best way to do this. Ask someone you trust, perhaps your minister or a church board member or an accountant. Failing that, simply call a couple of investment firms in your area and ask for the senior secretary. Tell her (yes, *her*—Wall Street is still male dominated) that you are a conservative, long-term investor and would appreciate her opinion on who would be the best person for you to talk to. Then call the suggested broker and ask for an appointment.

When you meet with the broker, ask how he or she does business and about his or her experience. Ask the same questions you would ask if hiring an employee. Tell the broker what you expect.

Brokers will also expect some things from you. They are selling their experience, knowledge, and time. If you use them, expect to pay for them. Many people will take a broker's time and advice and then execute their own transactions with discounters and no-load funds. This is a tough way to build a long-term relationship. And believe me, a broker will pick up on this very quickly. Courtesy and ethics go both ways. Take all the broker's time you need, but only what you need. Treat their time as you do your attorney's or accountant's and you'll have no problems.

When first approaching your broker, be *very* clear about what you want. I'm constantly amazed how many people tell me they want long-term investments but then want to fire me because I don't call with suggested changes each month. Many investors would do well to really analyze their past investing activities *before* telling a broker their philosophies. And rolling three-month CDs for the past five years is *not* being a long-term investor! It's being a short-term investor for a very long time.

Every broker expects to take some heat for ideas that don't work out, but no broker wants to be blamed for mistakes you make. I've had clients reject my first ten suggestions and question my judgment when they agreed to the eleventh and it didn't work out. They forget the first ten they passed up and only remember the eleventh. This kind of attitude will damage any relationship. Brokers make mistakes and clients make mistakes. We're all fallible.

Many "full service" brokers today can offer a discounted price on some of their commissions. If you want to go this route, I would simply ask that you be prepared to tell the broker what services you are willing to do without. It's increasingly expensive for a broker to figure out what's going on in the financial world, and at times investors' concerns about costs, however legitimate, can cause essential research and services to suffer.

Conflicts of Interest

Investment firms deal with conflicts of interest each day, sometimes successfully, sometimes not. These conflicts are complex enough that John L. Casey, Managing Director of Scudder, Stevens, and Clark, has written a book on the subject. (See resource center.) But unless you subscribe to our "ethical investing" concepts, brokers' conflicts of interest basically fall into three general categories: finding investments for the clients, selling securities for corporations and governments, and making money for ourselves.

Corporations and governments issuing securities want high prices; buyers want low ones. "Taking care of the client" can have one meaning for the finance people in New York and quite another to the broker in the local office when these two interests are weighed. And investment firms earn fees on virtually all transactions. Thus, you should always consider why the seller wants to sell and why you disagree and want to buy; and you should have a reasonably good idea of what's in it for the investment firm.

Brokers who understand the conflicts inherent in the business can help. Many don't care to acknowledge that conflicts exist, however, so they can hardly be expected to handle them.

Conflicts exist in more than just the investment firm's pricing of offerings. For example, excessive trading in and out creates large amounts of commissions; this process is called "churning." Some investments offer particularly high commissions to buy, and during a slow month at the firm these can look good to a broker. Plus, the broker's portion of the commission charge (versus the portion kept by the investment firm) is higher with some products than with other investments.

These would be tough for a saint to handle, much less someone trying to make a living. Understanding this can help you assure that these conflicts don't work to your detriment. They also help you really appreciate the broker who does care.

On the other hand, I have had clients reject good advice because they were overly sensitive that I would make a commission if they followed it. If that barrier exists between you and your advisor, you should seriously consider finding another broker or planner. Neither of you are benefiting from the relationship. In cases like this you should probably consider finding a fee-based planner or a money manager.

Fee-Based Money Management

A money manager is a professional who handles clients' investments for an annual fee. Money managers are employed through banks, investment firms, or as individuals and offer a real service for those who have special needs. For example, some managers will screen investments away from your portfolio that might conflict with your ethical values, as we've discussed. Unlike most mutual funds, managers can tailor a portfolio to suit your specifications and then consult with you about its progress.

That has a price of course—usually around 1% of your assets each year. In addition you must pay brokerage commissions too. Some investment firms are combining the two into a "wrap fee," usually around 3% per year. That is pretty high considering the stock market has averaged about 10% (before deducting fees and commissions) over the last fifty years, and bonds and money markets have done considerably less. Giving up what could easily be 30% of your returns seems a bit steep. I believe long-term investors who desire an account balanced with bonds and money market investments are better off avoiding the wrap fee and negotiating the commissions with the broker. It may be fine for a smaller (say $100,000 and under) active stock account however. Some very good money managers, who normally have multimillion-dollar minimums, are available to smaller investors through some wrap-fee programs from brokers. These are worth weighing against the costs.

Exercise caution when evaluating the track records of money managers. This is a fairly unregulated area, and there are several creative techniques to make track records look better than they really are. Always evaluate YOUR particular portfolio manager, not just the firm in general. I've had clients who employed the services of very fine, experienced firms, only to have their portfolios assigned to a recent business school graduate who was given great latitude. Perhaps most importantly, check out the manager's investment style and make sure it's the same as yours. A manager can have a great track record as a trader but fall apart when asked to invest conservatively for the long-run.

Investors who use a money manager should look beneath the yields promoted and see how those yields were achieved. Many engage in short-term trading, options strategies, and junk bond dealings for their clients. Corporations that abhor being pressured to produce earnings each quarter at the expense of long-term results should make sure their own pension fund managers aren't pressuring other corporations to do exactly that. Churches that detest lay-offs from leveraged corporations gone sour should question whether their own money managers buy junk bonds with their pension and endowment funds.

If you like the idea of social screening, you should be aware that not all money managers welcome the approach. It's a nuisance to many. They don't mind making subjective judgments about dozens of unusual financial ratios in a company's balance sheet, but they may feel that trying to determine whether the company produces something of value is too subjective. They often argue that you're bound to suffer if you screen certain companies away. I might agree with the latter . . . if they could show me studies that confirm that unethical companies prosper in the long run. Some say to invest regularly and donate some profit to charity. I'll agree . . . if they show me the passage that says Christians can prosper any way we like if we tithe.

What Would the Minister Do?

The best salesman I ever heard represented a company that drilled oil and gas wells for investors. He could quote industry statistics for hours about the economics of drilling. He almost had me reaching for my checkbook.

But I always stop and do an in-depth evaluation of a company's track record. And when I checked out this one, it appeared that they couldn't find oil and gas in a Chevron station!

Generic sales presentations can be deadly to your financial success, and they are widely used today. It's critical that you be very specific about your investments. One way to do this is to ask yourself, "Would my pastor understand this investment and put money in it?"

Now, your minister probably isn't a financial guru, but your perceptions of your minister's view can keep your investing conservative, simple, and ethical. For example, with this in mind you probably wouldn't buy the drilling partnership, but you might buy stock in a blue-chip, environmentally sensitive oil company. This simple technique can help you avoid a lot of pitfalls.

Mutual Funds as Counselors

A mutual fund is simply another form of money manager. But the most important thing I've learned over the years is that the Fidelitys, Merrill Lynchs, and other financial institutions of the world do not manage money; *people* at these institutions do. All you are doing when you buy a mutual fund is hiring an employee to manage your money and spread it across several investments. Some of these people know what they are doing, and some don't. Most mutual fund groups in the country have a combination of both. (Some are almost managed by committee and the individual is not as important. The American Fund, for example, employs a "multiple manager system.") It is usually important to get acquainted with the individual managing a fund before you buy it. Look at the manager's track record. Also, be sure that the person(s) who created any track record you're analyzing is still managing the fund. (Funds are not required to tell you when the manager is replaced.)

I tend to use funds as I increase the risks of my investments. I see little reason to buy "midget Ginnie Macs" through a fund, but I do use funds if I decide to purchase growth stocks or invest internationally. The professional management and diversification they offer make the costs of management acceptable.

Independent Counsel

"Independents" are planners and brokers who do not work for larger investment firms and banks, and there are many around today. Like the other financial advisors, they have advantages and disadvantages. Their main advantage is that they usually don't have their own mutual funds or programs they are encouraged to sell and can be more objective about the investments they recommend—an advantage in today's world of store-brand financial products. Also, some specialize in a particular field and can offer improved levels of competency.

Choosing the wrong independents can hurt you, of course. Because the major firms won't handle junk municipal bonds and penny stocks, these are a ripe area for independents. For example, most hotels in Florida offer daily seminars by small investment firms that specialize in junk municipal bonds, telling about the wonders of tax-free bonds paying incredible interest rates. Most seminars disclose the fact that only "4% of all municipal bonds defaulted during the great Depression." What they don't tell you is that the type of bonds they are promoting are the 4% that did. Some independents also specialize in penny stocks. Definitely avoid these.

If you do consider going with an independent, try to ascertain whether the person is independent for positive reasons or negative ones.

Cynical Counselors

I recently attended a two-hour financial seminar where the speaker spent ninety minutes citing "rip-off" tactics of banks, brokers, mortgage lenders, insurance companies, and others. (One of the things the speaker warned about was the 3% sales charge of using some Fidelity mutual funds.) The rest of the program was largely a presentation of creative means for creating tax deductions. Most of it was legal, but ethically reprehensible. The very limited investment part of the plan was a simplified version of what Wall Street calls "asset allocation" between stocks, bonds, and money market funds: meaning, you just switch your money around by watching one basic economic indicator and you never

242

lose money . . . simple. (I know Mr. Templeton and Mr. Lynch will be thrilled that their jobs have been made so easy and that they'll never have to lose money again!) This has been a popular strategy since the crash of 1987, but has a spotty record, at best. But I've never, ever heard it described as a risk-free way to get wealthy before.

At the end of the "educational seminar" the speaker briefly mentioned that his company did offer "money management" for those who needed it, but that his company "wasn't interested in fees or commissions." I couldn't help asking if they were willing to do this simply because they liked us. He responded that they did charge "about 2% or 3% a year" for the service. So I asked why it was better to pay him 2% or 3% each year instead of paying Fidelity a one-time 3% commission to have Peter Lynch manage my money in the Magellan Fund. He replied that the 2% or 3% was "just to cover expenses and stuff." The "and stuff" is what bothered me!

My point is that you should beware of anyone whose only sales pitch is cynicism regarding what everyone else is doing. (I prefer those who spend their time describing why their approach is more valuable.) These presentations are used by many and are similar to the "pea under the shell game," copying the strategy of those sidewalk shysters who use quick handwork to draw your attention away from the shell you should be watching. This financial version uses fast talk to get you looking at what everyone else might possibly do to you so that you won't watch what is actually being done. Very effective stuff in a cynical society.

Florida seems to attract these types, although other states probably have their share. They lure investors by appealing to the darker side of human nature— cynicism, greed, and the paranoia that "everyone is ripping me off . . . I may as well do it to somcone else." I've seen people lose tens of millions of dollars in ventures such as "six-month Ginnie Maes," oil and gas deals, mortgage lending deals, and gold deals by listening to these sales pitches and investment schemes.

God speaks to us in many ways, and one very important way is the small voice called "common sense." That little voice often tells me that if an investment is really great, a sea of people on the Street could make a lot of commissions selling it. If it's so limited in quantity that the big firms can't offer it, I wonder why someone had to promote a seminar to let me in on it. If it can make such incredible returns with absolutely no risk, why aren't the promoters down at the bank borrowing to make themselves rich? And should I trust my affairs to those who openly advocate "do unto others before they do unto you"? Listening to that little voice when it says "be cautious as snakes but gentle as doves" seems to work very well.

Financial Planners

Financial planners come in two varieties: commission-based and fee-based. Usually they have attended a fairly rigorous course from the College for Financial Planning and received a Certified Financial Planner designation. If financial planners have a "CFP," you can be reasonably assured that they are knowledgeable about a broad array of financial areas. However, the course is no substitute for years of experience with investments and the markets. I've seen some pretty weak investment planning come wrapped in comprehensive financial plans.

Commission-based planners examine your financial situation and earn commissions by providing the investments they think you need. Fee-based planners charge a fee to examine your situation and advise you, but will not get involved in providing the investments you need. For obvious reasons, you can normally expect more objective advice from a fee-based planner. This does not mean that it is necessarily better advice however. I've seen some strange investment advice given by totally objective counselors.

Good financial planners can be valuable for the busy professional or for those with complicated financial situations. Their primary purpose is to put your "big picture" together by coordinating your insurance, investments, taxes, business interests, and other concerns.

The biggest problem is that financial planners have a vast amount of ground to cover. I began the CFP course but stopped when I realized I could barely keep up with the investments area alone. To understand what's involved, compare the financial world to the world of medicine. Planners are like general practitioners. If my family physician spots a problem, he refers me to a specialist. I would lose confidence in him if he told me he could handle my stomach problems, my eye problems, my dental problems . . . you get the idea. Yet I have seen investors rely entirely on planners who have backgrounds in tax or insurance but only a "textbook" knowledge of investments. That makes me nervous. The solution is to develop a list of your needs and prioritize them, then interview several planners and see how their backgrounds match up with your needs. Then determine if they're trying to be everything to everybody.

Despite the increased objectivity offered by fee-based planners, there can be problems too. For example, you have to pay a fee whether you do anything they suggest or not. Years ago I worked with a firm that charged $10,000 to do superb financial plans. It was widely known that many of their clients never got around to even changing their wills, much less following through on anything else. They paid the fee anyway.

Second, you may have to pay commissions on top of the planning fee if you do implement the ideas. This naturally increases the costs of your plan. To avoid that, some planners only recommend no-load plans. That may seem to address the matter of economy, but some superb investments come with a commission, so you're hardly ahead to ignore a universe of opportunities just so you don't have to pay commissions. You should be using a fee-based planner in order to hear an objective evaluation of the best investments possible, not to hear about just the ones that don't interfere with the planner's fee.

A few planners charge a fee to evaluate your situation, recommend no-load investments, and then charge an annual management fee to keep an eye on them for you. Unless you are getting some very valuable service or trading on a short-term basis, you will probably not be ahead if you save a one-time 4% sales charge but pay 1% each year for the life of your investment. Some mutual funds purchased through commission brokers and planners essentially do the same thing through "12 B-1 fees." Evaluate all these plans carefully.

Some planners charge a fee to evaluate your situation and then earn commissions if you implement their advice. This is like paying a salesperson to make a pitch. If there's an advantage to this, I don't know what it is. Most planners carry some advantage, but stick to the ones that only require one payment for services rendered. For example, a better arrangement is one where the planner earns a fee that is offset by any commissions you might generate in implementing the suggested plan.

One particular problem you should be aware of is that many financial planning firms have discovered that there is a limited market of people willing to pay a planning fee, so they have turned to commissions to supplement their fee income. In other words, the firm was founded as fee-based but later added commission services to stay in business. There is nothing wrong with this. However, some of these firms do a better job of describing the firm's former method of compensation rather than their current methods. This might conflict with your interests if you're still expecting an unbiased allocation of your money.

Cost IS important, but when focused on exclusively, much more important considerations, such as experience level, quality of service, and investment philosophy, are ignored. Your aim should be to find the most competent professional counsel who shares your investing philosophy, is easy to work with, and charges a reasonable fee, however it may be structured.

Accountants

Some investors depend heavily on their accountants for investment advice, which probably means one of two things: they have an exceptional accountant or an unexceptional investment advisor. I do know some accountants who are very knowledgeable about investments. But I know a lot more who should stick with taxes and accounting. Notable exceptions would be accounting firms with experts on staff who do financial planning for a fee.

If they do err, accountants generally err on the conservative side. For this reason, they can sometimes be a good check and balance if you or your investment counsel tend to be aggressive. Accountants are conservative by nature, at least when offering investment advice, but there can also be an element of self-interest in this approach. As a good friend once told me, "Clients don't thank me if I approve an investment that works, but they sure blame me for the ones that don't. It's safer not to approve any." It could be in your best interest to have a serious talk with your accountant about how comfortable he or she really is about giving investment advice.

Discount Brokerage Services

Discount brokers do not offer advice, so they are not usually regarded as counselors. (Essentially they "counsel" investors on the advantages of not seeking counsel.) They simply buy and sell stocks and bonds at a reduced commission rate. However, I have included them in this section because those who make their own investment decisions often rely on such services, in which case they should have a good one. In fact, I would use the services of a discounter occasionally if I were to leave this business.

Most discounters do a decent job during normal times, but some had severe difficulties during the crash of 1987. Forget those who simply advertise "cheap." You want savings and good execution capabilities, and there is no free lunch here either. To find the best discount services, the *Good Money* newsletter suggests you obtain a 44-page survey called "Discount Brokerage Commission Survey." (Send $11.95 to Mercer Financial Services, 80 Fifth Avenue, Suite 800, New York, New York 10011.)

The head of a large discount firm was recently quoted as saying, "Our passion is to make investors independent, not make them dependent on a commissioned salesman." I would be a lot more comfortable if he had said, "Our passion is to make investors successful and to help them avoid salesmen who are only interested in a commission." Advice from discounters to go it alone is not necessarily devoid of self-interest any more than the advice from brokers and planners to seek counsel.

Media Counsel

Various magazines, newspapers, and television shows also offer counsel on investment planning. Despite their reservations about the media in other areas, when it comes to financial matters some investors seem to feel that if it's in print, it must be true. That's as dangerous as blindly following any other advisor. (A warning I even make to you as you read *my* thoughts.)

Brokers and planners are a frequent target of financial writers, and often for good reason. But investors should understand that the financial media is not opposed to your paying *them*, in the form of subscription dollars, for advice. This potential self-interest can be clearly illustrated by using mutual funds as an example.

Financial publications feature many articles about the merits of load funds versus no-load funds, and most seem to favor no-load funds. Maybe these articles are intended to be totally objective, I don't know. But I do know that no-load funds spend a lot of advertising dollars in the financial media to spread the word about their funds, just as load funds spend a lot of commission dollars with brokers to spread their message.

You know by now that I find *Forbes* magazine informative reading, although they tend to glorify wealth too much as far as I'm concerned. But I want to cancel my subscription about every other month because they seem to feel a duty to counterbalance brokers' biases toward load products with their own biases toward no-load. In the 6 March 1989 issue there was a perfect example of this. They were examining the expanding world of junk bond mutual funds, and the article contained a chart showing that the four best-performing funds were load funds sold by brokers and the fifth-rated fund was a no-load fund. In a full-page analysis, the author compared the merits of the no-load to the demerits of a loaded fund. The discredited load fund wasn't one of the top four funds however, but a poor performer sold only by one investment firm. The writer had several theories about why load funds outsell no-load funds, but the superior performance of the four load funds wasn't one of them. In fact, if the top-performing funds had any merit, they weren't mentioned in the article.

I pick on *Forbes* only because I respect it enough to study it weekly. Other magazines editorialize in favor of their advertisers much more blatantly. And I do believe *Forbes should* examine why the investment firm mentioned in the above article sells its store-brand fund rather than others (or sells any junk bond fund for that matter). But the magazine might serve the readers better if the editors and writers provided a small amount of insight into the very top performing funds, rather than confining themselves to elaborating extensively on the merits of the fifth-rated, no-load fund.

I also respect *The Wall Street Journal* and read it daily, but it is not above a similar type of journalism occasionally. One of the best examples I can cite was on the front page on 13 March 1989 in an article about complaints investors had filed against brokers who misled them about mutual funds during the past few years. Complaints centered on the investors not being aware that 1) the funds fluctuated in value; 2) contained commissions that were often "hidden"; 3) could pay an interest rate that would vary if interest rates changed. The article contained quotes from investors such as retired schoolteachers and ended with: "She says she will never buy through a broker again." It also included some distorted statistics implying that no-load sales (like the kind advertised in the back of *The Wall Street Journal*) are booming while load funds sold by brokers are suffering terribly.

I have absolutely no doubt that many of the stories cited are true. But there are other stories—the kind you rarely read about—that are also enlightening. For example, a retired gentleman called me during the falling interest rate period of the mid-1980s and said he couldn't live on the interest paid by certificates of deposit any more. He wanted me to evaluate his situation and make suggestions. He asked if I would meet him in his local library to discuss the matter. We spent a few hours together the first day, and I took his financial information with me to analyze. About a week later I called him back and we got together again at the library, at his request. I spent a couple more hours explaining what I had found and suggested that he consider a good government bond fund for part of his money.

I called him a week later, and he said he'd taken my advice and bought a government bond fund. He said he saw no reason to pay me a commission and had looked in the back of *The Wall Street Journal* and found a no-load fund that promised a high rate. Naturally I saw little reason to stay in touch with the man.

About two years later, government bonds were paying 7%, though most funds were quoting yesterday's returns which were considerably higher. (This problem was actually caused by government regulations about the way funds advertise yields.) I decided there was little reason to remain in these funds and advised my clients of such.

About a year after that, when government bonds had declined substantially in price, the man called me again. He said his fund was performing poorly and he couldn't understand why I had thought it was a good idea to buy one. He wanted my advice on other investments, but he still couldn't see any reason to pay a commission (or pay for my time).

The Moral of the Story

There's a moral here that can help you (and *The Wall Street Journal* too), for this is not an uncommon occurrence. I could tell you many, many other stories of a similar nature.

First, don't take a broker's time to evaluate your situation, listen to the suggestions, take the advice, and then give your investment business to someone else. You are hardly encouraging a relationship of mutual trust and interest if you sit in a broker's office and demand to be offered investments where you don't think the broker can make any money (though the *Journal* actually used this to illustrate how abusive brokers can be). Brokers shouldn't hide their fees, but they might be tempted to rationalize that you deserve to be deceived if you demand their services for nothing. You expect to be paid for your work and experience and so does a broker.

Second, people were hurt by buying funds from the back of *The Wall Street Journal,* too, but somehow the author didn't see fit to mention that.

Third, many people were enticed to enter funds at the low point of interest rates because mutual funds were allowed to advertise through papers (and quote through brokers) exaggerated interest rates during that period. I, and several other brokers I know, did seminars and mailings on those exaggerated claims. Isn't that worth a mention?

In fairness, newspapers do usually have policies about not commenting on the merits of the ads they run each day. They simply display what they are paid to advertise with the copy provided them (the convenient supermarket concept again). However, while this may be appropriate for my local paper which advertises everything and anything, doesn't it seem that the financial press, which specializes in that one area, might bear greater responsibility? After all, the ads they are running carry information that will directly affect their subscribers, who are reading them for information about that very area. Couldn't their analysts look at the claims in the paper as well as the claims of brokers?

Articles such as this are too little, too late for the investor. Worse, they can create a wall of cynicism between investors and any professional counsel they might need. It's all right with me if the media cautions readers about all the land mines out there today—just as long as they don't imply that the only mine detector an investor needs is a renewed subscription.

Advertising Counsel

Have you ever noticed that the analytical editorial space of many publications is usually surrounded by equally analytical advertising? In doing this, marketing departments use the fear and greed of the moment to promote what you might buy (called "shooting while the ducks are flying"), which may or may not be in your best interest. For example, before the crash of 1987 stock-related investment ads proliferated, promoting the large returns investors had enjoyed over the past few years. After the crash they disappeared, only to be replaced by ads for money market funds, certificates of deposit, and government bonds stressing safety. Almost two years later, the stock-related ads are coming back.

By following those ads you would have gotten in at the top, out at the bottom, avoided a market that has been very good (at least for two years), and be tempted to try it all over again at much higher prices. Ads are placed with the objective of increasing the advertiser's market share, not of promoting your well-being. Several studies indicate that you can actually be guided to good investments by watching what is not advertised and avoid bad investments by ignoring what is heavily advertised! Be aware of this when reading the various financial publications (or listening to other counselors).

Media Fear

One last problem with taking counsel from the media is that reading the headlines can paralyze you with fear. A classic ad run by *The New York Times* illustrates my point. It showed a small, intimidated man sitting on a world with a crack down the middle. The caption beneath read, "These times demand the *Times*." With all due respect to a great newspaper, I'll probably survive if I don't happen to read it tomorrow. "All the news that's fit to print" may not be all *that* important. The point for investors is that fear makes money for people selling papers, but it won't do much for you.

Most problems create opportunities if you can offer solutions.

There will never be a time when there is nothing to worry about. During the early 1980s papers expressed deep concern about our high unemployment. Are they comfortable now that the government says unemployment is near an all-time low? No. Because now there's a labor shortage! And full employment will create inflation! Investors will benefit by realizing that most problems create opportunities if you can offer a solution, and these problems are a staple offering of the media. The answer is to keep them in perspective.

Newsletters

You can also subscribe to an investment newsletter for additional information about investing, and there are dozens to choose from. This area is also unregulated, so you can definitely expect advertised track records to be somewhat creative. Some can add value to your investing, but most seem to be of interest to those investors seeking short-term opportunities.

Mark Hulbert, a *Forbes* columnist who tracks the records of investment newsletters, recently said that only 11 out of over 100 newsletters evaluated over time actually outperformed the market averages. This was largely due to the commission costs of moving around as much as the newsletters suggested. He also did a study which indicated that the stocks favored by newsletter writers provided a 43.6% gain (about market average) over 25 months before transaction costs, but only 20.2% when costs were factored in.[2] I personally believe this is the reason I've seen so many people grow disenchanted with the promises of newsletters. Most of us should probably spend more time with the Bible and less with stock tip sheets if we would truly prosper! However, some newsletters are good for the long-term,

---

2 *Forbes* (16 April 1990): 182.

conservative investor and some specialize in the ethical investing area. (See the resource section.)

Christian Planners

An increasing number of "Christian" financial planners have come on the scene in recent years. That could be good news IF they truly apply the principles of the faith and don't just quote them, and IF they have the financial expertise required.

I hate to admit it, but some of the worse plans I have seen have been developed by planners who are very obvious about their faith. Yet the only faith obvious in some of the plans was a need for God to work a miracle to make them work!

You do not need a Christian financial planner. You need a financial plan based on Christian principles.

Since they have identified their businesses with the Christian faith, I personally believe that we should hold Christian planners to a higher level of accountability. We should expect their plans to look somewhat different from most plans the world offers us; and we should certainly expect a higher level of ethical awareness on their part. I also believe we should expect them to donate some time (and possibly some income) to the work of God.

For example, lecturing to the not-so-wealthy about wills is as important as lecturing to wealthy Christians about managing money. I also believe any Christian financial planner should know the efficient means available through charities and religious denominations for supporting their work. I have been disappointed to find that several books I've read on the subject of "Christians and finances" have devoted most of their time to the subject of "Christian getting" and little to "Christian giving."

You do not need a Christian financial planner. You need a financial plan based on Christian principles.

Christian financial planners who serve ALL Christians attempt to understand how each investment affects humanity, truly incorporate the vehicles that fund the spread of God's Word, honestly disclose their compensation structure, and know what other Christians and Christian organizations can do with your money. They should also be experienced, knowledgeable, and subject to the same scrutiny as you would use with any advisor.

If they offer all the above, they are well worth considering as a counselor. If they offer simplistic solutions that encourage self-centered accumulation, they may be one of the worst people you can consider as a counselor.

I am pleased that more and more Christians are finding that the principles of faith can, and must, be applied from Monday through Friday. But I also feel that there's entirely too much "I'm a Christian and you can blindly trust me" in the professions today. As I said before, there are as many verses in the Bible about diligence (and false prophets) as there are on the value of counsel.

But if you do decide to go this way, remember you aren't looking for Christ to manage your money. You're looking for a Christian, subject to all the human weaknesses we all have. Help them do their best through your understanding of their business.

Conclusions

Search for counselors as you would for employees. They don't just pop up on the golf course, on magazine racks, or at hotel seminars. Like investments, the ones you want probably have to be searched for, while the ones you don't want will come looking for you. An ideal counselor must stand between you and the many, many influences from the investment community, banking community, financial press, and electronic media that would vie for your money, not all of which conform to either common sense or Christian principles.

Pay particular attention to the biblical teaching that says "by their works you will know them." That's an ancient way of saying, "Don't worry about their ethical standards; worry about their ethical behavior." We live in an age where images are created by commercials, brochures, and public relations machines. These may reflect the work the person is engaged in, but can often disguise any weaknesses in the work itself. (Remember how many commercials focused on trust, safety, strength, and wisdom after the crash of 1987?) There are few areas where being able to distinguish between "style" and "substance" is more rewarding than in financial advertising. Look deeper than first impressions.

After you find good counsel, remember that your relationship can be somewhat like a marriage. For example, since I've been married I no longer eat too much . . . my wife feeds me too much. Similarly, according to my clients, I sell them the investments that go down . . . they buy the ones that go up. It's a subtle difference and a basic part of human nature, but it causes a lot of financial divorces.

Competent, honest planners do not work for nothing. But they will disclose costs to you and will be aware of inevitable conflicts of interest. My personal experience leads me to believe that conflicts of interest are rarely absent from the financial scene. Just make sure your planner is balanced and fair.

Use as many of these counselors as necessary, but understand that the more advice you seek from those who desire your fees, commissions, and subscription fees, the more confused you might become. Try to decide what you really want from your counselor and stick with it.

Financial deregulation and its subsequent increased awareness has everyone doing everything. The financial supermarket tries to do all these things for all people. Financial reporters are now analysts and advisors. Banks are now investment brokers. Investment firms handle everything from CDs to airplanes. Fee-based counselors are earning compensation that used to be called commissions. Insurance agents are suddenly financial planners. All this might be beneficial for investors— or it may just confuse them more. The jury is still out. (I'll render my one prediction of the future here . . . financial supermarkets will look more like health food stores in the 1990s. It may happen too slowly, but it will happen.)

But there is no question that you are being subjected to more financial influence than ever before. So seek out those who will guide your money into a few solid areas where it does good work and where you don't need to worry about it daily. Fear, anxiety, and risk certainly cannot be eliminated in today's world, but they can be minimized. Greed, however, should be eradicated.

Above all, remember your own principles and standards as you listen to the counselors you deem necessary. Seek out those whose advice reflects the honesty, humanity, and patience advocated by your faith . . . whether they call themselves Christian or not.

259

You and Your Financial Advisor

DON'T...

1. Expect free advice.

2. Listen to too many voices.

3. Expect your advisor to be infallible.

Do...

1. Research any potential advisor thoroughly.

2. Understand the priorities good advisors must establish for their time.

3. Look for an advisor who reflects your principles and standards, both in investment philosophy and in ethical considerations.

4. Understand that good advisors will recommend ideas that seem unpopular at the moment. They are working against advertising, articles, newscasts, your neighbor, and even your own feelings when doing this.

11

The Joy of Planned Giving

Never hesitate to hold out your hand; never hesitate to accept the outstretched hand of another.

Pope John XXIII

THE PARABLE OF THE GOOD SAMARITAN is a crucial passage of Scripture for modern Christians, containing truth that is as up-to-date for us as it was for those to whom Jesus told it.

First, those who passed by the wounded man were respected and religious persons, in a hurry to get somewhere. Second, the man in need didn't have to ask for help to receive it. Third, Jesus did not make the homes or synagogues of the priest and Levite the setting for his parable. He knew how easy it is to miss neighbors in need by staying within our own little worlds. He thrust them out onto the road of life, out of warm and familiar settings, where each would have the opportunity to meet his neighbor. Fourth, the Samaritan used his time and talents to provide for his neighbor's immediate needs; but the Samaritan also left money to assure that the man would be cared for long after the Samaritan had gone.

For me, these four concepts summarize both the concerns and mission of "planned giving."

Acquired Abundance

Over the past decade I have been privileged to work with several hundred prosperous retirees in Florida, and again and again I have observed them grappling with the shock and surprise of two facts: first, that the American dream of golfing and fishing every day doesn't make them as happy as they had imagined it would; and second, that having money can create as many problems, both financially and spiritually, as not having any money.

Financially, I disagree. Having money is a blessing when you understand it. Spiritually, I agree. Trying to keep money can indeed be as much of a spiritual problem as trying to get it.

Millions of Americans seem to be chasing their fortunes, with very little idea of what they'll do when they catch them. We quote phrases such as "you can't take it with you" and "money can't buy happiness," but we don't really operate that way. We don't think about what accumulated money can or should mean for us as Christians.

I believe accumulated money should do three things.

First, it should provide us with all the security that is possible from worldly assets. Money can only go so far in providing security and peace of mind, but it IS necessary for the basic needs of food and shelter (and even golf balls!).

Second, accumulated money should be invested so that it does what it can for others. As investors, we control a large pool of productive resources. It is our responsibility to consider how those resources affect humanity as well as how much return they produce for us, especially since we've learned how interdependent the two aspects can be.

Third, accumulated money should be given slowly over the years, or as a one-time estate settlement, to those people, churches, and charities we love. Proper planning can make this as efficient as possible.

Planned Giving Versus Estate Planning

Estate planning is the efficient distribution of our assets to children, churches, charities, and others we love. Planned giving is the efficient distribution of assets specifically to the churches, schools, and charities we care about. Estate planning can reduce taxes and administrative expenses. Planned giving can do the same. It's been said that estate planning does nothing for us; it is done entirely for our heirs. Not so with planned giving. It does some wonderful things for the churches, schools, and charities we love; but it can do some wonderful things for us too.

Planned giving is what its name implies: you simply plan to give in the future. This requires the expertise of a professional of one kind or another, and it can be very simple or very complex depending on what you would like to accomplish. It is a complement to, not a replacement for, your regular, ongoing support of the causes you care for.

Planned giving is particularly effective for three groups of people: those with modest assets but a desire to give, those with appreciated assets, and those who need assets dependably managed for them.

Giving from Your Estate

The simplest, most widely used planned gift is the inclusion of your church or charity in your will. An attorney can help you with this, either when drawing up your will or through the addition of an amendment called a codicil. Some people decide on a certain dollar amount for each cause. Some leave a percentage of their estate. I've even seen people "tithe their estate" and leave 10% to their church. Those with greater wealth sometimes leave what they can tax-free to their children and bequeath the remainder tax-free to churches and charities.

If you have an estate of any size at all, one of the hardest questions you'll have to answer during your lifetime is how much money you should leave your children. Some parents simply leave as much as possible without thinking about it. It's not even unusual in our society to feel that the size of our estate is somehow a measure of the value of our lives. Yet the values and lives of many children have been damaged by the prospects of or actual receipt of a substantial inheritance. (Some of the more obvious examples that come to mind are regularly featured, often tragically, in the pages of *People* magazine and other purveyors of popular culture.)

One of the hardest questions you'll have to answer during your lifetime is how much money you should leave your children.

"Making it on our own," through the grace of God, is one of the things my wife and I most cherish, so we had to think about that a long time when deciding how much to leave our son and how to structure it. This became doubly important because we also want to leave him a testimony about what we think about charity, about our neighbors, and about our church. Despite my own personal experience and my assisting others with these decisions, I really can't tell you what is right for you. I only suggest that you seriously question the prevalent notion that the fullest expression of love for your children is leaving them the largest estate possible.

Pre-Planning Your Estate

In an earlier chapter I mentioned that one stage of our financial lives concerns the "conversion" of growth assets into assets that pay us an income during retirement. There can be significant advantages to you if you make your giving plans prior to converting these assets. Most stocks, real estate, and other appreciated assets are simply sold. Capital gains taxes are paid, and the remainder is reinvested in such things as government bonds that produce income. However, planned giving offers several ways to do the conversion so assets can be sold and reinvested without being subject to the reduction of capital gains taxes.

Pooled Income Funds

The first involves the use of a "pooled income fund," which is simply a mutual fund operated by a church or charity. For example, my denomination has a fund of a few million dollars invested in government bonds. The Chemical Bank purchases and holds the bonds for our investors and sends regular checks out just like any mutual fund would. You can get in the fund (without commission) by simply sending a check to the church's headquarters.

My denomination currently pays all the expenses of operating the fund, which is somewhat unusual, so your income isn't reduced by management fees. You are relieved of making investment decisions and are assured of a steady, safe income for life. You also get an income tax deduction to use now, based on your age, since the money is distributed to the church at your death (or the death of your spouse, if joint income is desired). This plan also avoids the delays and expenses of probate so the church receives the full value of your gift.

You can benefit even more by donating appreciated stocks. For example, assume you own 100 shares of IBM bought years ago at $30 per share. It's currently worth $120 per share. You are concerned about a market decline and you really need more than the 3% income it pays, but you would have to pay tax on the gains of $90 per share if you sold it.

If you send the stock to a pooled income fund, they could sell it without the capital gains tax being due, the full amount of the proceeds would then be invested, you would get an immediate tax deduction based on your age, and you would have gained a larger income for the rest of your life. You avoid tax on the gains, therefore receiving a larger, secure income for life; avoid any drop the stock might experience; get a tax deduction; are relieved of management responsibilities; and support your church without the expense and delay of probate. This is accomplished by simply sending your stock to the church's pooled income fund rather than to your broker (this may be one reason many planners and brokers aren't familiar with the program). You can usually designate that the money remaining at your death be divided any way you choose among your local church, regional church groups, or your denomination's national programs. Some funds will even send a portion to other charities or schools. My suggestion is that you not overdo that provision if they manage the money for you.

Many denominations and charities operate such a program. Ask your pastor or charity contact if such a program exists. But since most of the clergy are more interested in the spiritual side of the work, they may not even be aware of such programs. In the resource center at the back I have included some addresses of different denominations and organizations where you can write for information. They can usually provide you with a computer illustration of what the fund will do for your present income and tax picture, as well as for what it will do for your church or charity after you're gone.

Most programs work best when your desire to give comes first and your profit motive comes second.

Be aware that these benefits encourage some advisors to promote the economics of planned giving without particular concern for the charitable intent. My opinion is that the intent should be there before pursuing most planned giving programs. There are times when the economic merits can stand on their own, but most programs work best when your desire to give comes first and your profit motive comes second. Besides, I think God would prefer it that way—and I'm certain that Congress does. I have learned over the years to be wary of investments and programs that are simply put together to keep a few dollars out of the coffers of the IRS. I would hate to explain some bad intent to the IRS down the road. And explaining to God would be even tougher!

Charitable Gift Annuities

Pooled income funds provide a stable income, but this income can fluctuate over time if interest rates change. You may want to consider a "charitable gift annuity" if you prefer a fixed income. Rather than directing your money or appreciated securities into a mutual fund, this vehicle directs it to an insurance company, often operated by the denomination, which can guarantee an income for life that will not fluctuate. Some foundations back these annuities with their own assets. Another advantage is that your church or charity can often receive an immediate donation of a portion of your gift. There are slightly different tax ramifications than with a pooled income fund, so you need to request a personalized illustration from your giving contact about what this plan can do for you and your church. Many churches and charities have the ability to provide this. Once again you may have to look around a bit to find someone knowledgeable about it.

269

Charitable Remainder Trusts

These are for people who like the advantages offered by the pooled income fund and the charitable gift annuity but prefer to manage their own investments. They have their attorney set up a trust which pays them while they live (and usually their spouse and sometimes their children who survive them) but distributes remaining monies to their church or charity when they die. They can deposit appreciated assets, such as stocks or real estate, into the trust and sell them without taxes on the gain. They also receive an immediate tax deduction which varies with their particular situation. When the securities are sold, the full proceeds can be reinvested into various securities that can provide income and be managed for capital gains. Anything remaining at the death of the last beneficiary will go to specified church organizations without the expense and delays of probate. Cash and non-appreciated securities may also be used.

The expense of having an attorney set up a trust makes them appropriate for those with larger gifts in mind—$50,000 and up is normally quoted. Some churches and charities have attorneys on retainer and are willing to pay part or all of the expense of setting up a trust.

Charitable remainder trusts aren't particularly difficult to set up and manage, but many attorneys are unfamiliar with them, so you may want to deal with a specialist. The flexibility and relative simplicity of these trusts have made them very popular lately. I consider them very powerful financial tools that are too often ignored. They come in two forms: a "unitrust" pays a variable income each year and an "annuity" trust pays a set amount. You may name yourself, a charity employee or department, a friend, or a trust department to be your trustee (that is, to manage the money).

Foundations

Other vehicles such as private foundations can be of particular interest to those with even more substantial assets. Most churches and charities have people who can fill you in on those, and most national accounting firms are knowledgeable on the subject, as are most tax attorneys, estate planning attorneys, and large bank

> **APPRECIATED ASSETS.** Those assets, such as stocks or real estate, which have gone up in value and would cause a tax if sold.

trust departments. You may also write the Council on Foundations at 1828 L. Street N.W., Washington, D.C., 20036-5168 for information.

Giving Through Insurance

Insurance company contracts are another approach that can offer substantial benefits to those desiring to give. I like to divide this area into two parts: contracts that exist and those you can create.

Using Current Policies

People buy life insurance when they are younger as protection for loved ones in the event of the early death of a provider. When they reach retirement and do not need the death benefit to educate children or pay off mortgages, many people simply change the beneficiary of the policy to leave part or all of the proceeds to their church. This may create a tax deduction if the change is irrevocable, and proceeds are paid without probate. The process is simple. Just write your company for a "change of beneficiary" form.

Other people buy annuities during their peak earning years, discover they have sufficient income during retirement, and do not withdraw the interest they have

271

earned. They can simply write their insurance company and make the beneficiary their church or charity. There is a particular advantage to this since all the taxes on the accumulated interest are essentially forgiven when the church or charity receives the gift. This may sound like an aggressive tax strategy to you at first but it really isn't. You could own a CD all those years and donate the interest earned to the church each year. This creates a tax deduction and essentially makes the interest tax-free. The only difference with the annuity is that you have maintained control of the interest in case you need it later.

Creating Policies

Some people like to make a fairly substantial gift to their church without a large outlay. This can be done by creating a life insurance policy. You can contact any competent insurance agent and arrange this. I usually like term policies for this since we are not particularly interested in the savings feature other policies may offer. The payments can be tax deductible if the church owns the policy and is not just the beneficiary. Ask your agent for details.

If you feel you may need to access some savings in later years, you could consider creating an annuity with the church as beneficiary. You don't have the large immediate death benefit, as you do with a life insurance policy, but you will accumulate more savings for possible access. Your money accrues without income taxes until you need to withdraw any of the interest earned. Money you do not withdraw goes to the church without income taxes or probate. A different form of policy may be appropriate if you are more certain your cash needs will not be high.

Irrevocable planned gifts, such as the pooled income fund, gift annuity, and charitable trust, provide an immediate income tax deduction for your gift. This annuity plan with the church as beneficiary does not, since you can use your money or change the beneficiary at any time. The income tax deduction is traded for the ability to maintain control of the money in case of emergency. It is a good plan to consider for money you may need in the future. The other plans are for money you won't need back (though any income payments are yours of course).

Gifting a Home

A home is a significant part of most people's assets, so there may be advantages in looking into giving this asset to your church (some also give vacation homes). As I have mentioned, I often work with retirees in Florida, many of whom have families up north who will receive most of their estates. One problem that frequently arises is what to do with the home when the retiree passes away. It's not always easy for out-of-state heirs to coordinate the sale of a home. Many retirees also worry about what would happen to their homes if they had to move to a retirement or nursing facility.

Retaining a Life Interest

Some give their home to the church now but retain what's called a "life interest." This simply means they have complete control and use of their home as long as they live. They can include a clause in the arrangement which gives their pastor or another trusted person the authority to sell the home and use the proceeds to care for them should they have to enter a nursing home. Upon their death, the home, or what is left of sale proceeds, goes to the church without probate. The donor gets an immediate income tax deduction for the portion expected to go to charity. This requires the use of an attorney who is knowledgeable on the subject, but it isn't all that complicated.

Gifting Qualified Plans

Many Christians have substantial Individual Retirement Accounts, Keoghs, and pension plans. Should they not need all the money they have accumulated in these plans, they can make their church the beneficiary by simply writing the trustee of their plan. Again, this can be a significant tax advantage because the deferred tax liability is essentially forgiven. You maintain control of the funds until your death, so there's no immediate income tax deduction. Proceeds are paid without probate.

Gifting Appreciated Assets

Another simple but often overlooked plan is to give appreciated assets to the church for your regular support. For example, assume you paid $2,000 for a security, held it for more than a year, and it's now worth $5,000. You could sell it and realize a $3,000 gain. Assuming you are in the 28% tax bracket, you would owe $840 in taxes on the gain. That would leave you with $4,160 to give to the church (and deduct as a charitable contribution). A better approach might be to give the stock to the church and have them sell it. They would pay no capital gains tax, would get the full $5,000, and you could deduct $5,000 as a charitable contribution. A good deal.

Note: This can create a "preference item" for a very few taxpayers. Check with tax counsel if you pay "alternative minimum tax."

Giving Strategies

The economics of planned giving are strongest when you have a deferred tax liability you are not looking forward to paying. Also, you can give more efficient financial support to the church's current work by giving appreciated securities. You should consider income funds, gift annuities, and charitable trusts when converting appreciated securities and real estate into income-producing assets. From a tax standpoint, you might consider leaving assets with potential tax liabilities (such as IRAs, Keoghs, and pension plan assets) to your church or charities and leave assets (such as money market funds and certificates of deposit) that have no deferred tax liability to children. I often see people do the opposite: they leave the IRAs and annuities to their children simply because they have been the long-standing beneficiaries and leave a cash gift to their church. Think seriously about reversing this.

Efficient giving allows you to give even more support to the causes you care about without actually costing you more. In other words, you get more for your money. It just takes planning.

Dependable Management

Those without appreciated assets usually cite the attraction of having their assets managed for them as a reason to consider the more basic planned giving programs. For example, it can be a relief to have someone, like the Chemical Bank I mentioned, manage high quality investments for you. There is no need to search for the highest rates every six months, talk with brokers and planners about the prospects of the markets, or involve your attorney in complicated estate planning. Some churches and charities will even

275

manage a "revocable trust"—where you may not even leave the money to the charity—should you simply want their expertise. A simple way to avoid a lot of stress (not to mention expense).

A Balancing Act of Love

It is very important that you discuss your planned giving with your children or other heirs. They need to understand why you want to remember your church and charities. Great harm can be done when disgruntled family members do not understand and therefore misread your real feelings and intentions. At the very least, explain your feelings and desires to them in a letter to be read after your death.

The distribution of estate assets is always a balancing act of love. One very useful tool to consider is what is known as "wealth replacement."

Assume you have $20,000 worth of appreciated stock you would like to convert into income-producing bonds. You want to remember your church and you could use the extra income, but you do not want to remove such a large amount from your children's inheritance. Actually, you can accomplish all three.

Remember, I said you get an immediate tax deduction with some of the plans we discussed. This deduction is a current benefit you will not enjoy if you do not use the planned giving approach, so you might want to use this tax deduction for your heirs' benefit.

For example, assume an analysis of your situation shows you will save $3,000 in taxes by using a pooled income fund rather than by simply selling the appreciated stock. You could then walk into a bank or investment firm and spend that $3,000 on a zero-coupon bond for your two-year-old granddaughter's college education. At 9%, your $3,000 will grow into $12,000 by the time she is ready for college. This can normally be done so it is tax-free, but you should consult tax counsel when larger gifts are involved. As a result, the pooled income fund provides you with a higher income during your lifetime (which can preserve other assets for heirs since you won't need to spend principal) without management worries; provides your church with a substantial gift at your death; and the zero-coupon bond purchased through tax savings helps your grandson or granddaughter with future college expenses. The education funding can actually be done with securities or life insurance contracts. The process is very simple and can be accomplished when using pooled income funds, gift annuities, and charitable trusts. That's a balancing act that makes everyone happy.

The essence of planned giving is your desire to support God's work; your desire to be as efficient as possible in doing it; and your desire to handle it so that family interests, charitable interests, and your interests are balanced, making it productive for everyone concerned. Isn't this a much more joyous way to handle money when compared to some of the battles over estates we've all witnessed over the years?

A Personal Request

Having served on several church finance committees and as a vestryman, I'd like to make a special appeal. Your church leaders spend a great deal of time with financial concerns. The needs are many and the resources are usually limited.

Discuss your giving plans with a member of your church finance committee or another church leader to see how your plans fit in with the needs of your church. This may help you see that you need to go in a different direction, or the leaders may be able to accommodate your plans by shifting their priorities a little.

In regard to the church itself, I would encourage financial officers not to use bequests and gifts for the normal operating budget of the church. While I would obviously make an exception in the case of a financially struggling church, I believe that as a rule substantial bequests can lead to financial complacency on the part of the congregation.

The purpose of bequests is to accomplish greater things . . . "above and beyond what we ask or think" . . . not to encourage regular contributors to withhold support from God's work.

An excellent way to accomplish that is to set up an "endowment fund" at your church. These often provide guidelines for how the money will be used and who will direct its use, and they are relatively simple to establish. Ask your church leaders to look into this if you don't have one already. Many regional and national church groups also have established funds that accept gifts of almost any size.

Planned Giving of Yourself

Some of the best planned giving you can do has nothing to do with money. I mentioned earlier that many Florida retirees are not happy just playing golf or fishing every day. Conversations with my clients over the years have proven to me that many would be happier if they felt more useful. I believe that Christians, who understand the concept of "servanthood" as the very ground of their being, particularly feel this way. All of us need to have hobbies and recreation, but we also must have a real purpose and be of value to others. Consider the planned giving of your time and talents to satisfy that need.

Attorneys could give their time to help fellow Christians with wills, trusts, and other legal details. Accountants could volunteer to help with tax preparation. Restauranteurs could assist in Meals on Wheels or other outreach programs for the elderly, the hungry, and the homeless. Outdoor buffs might work with an environmental group or lead nature hikes to teach others about the need to care for the glorious creation God has given us.

Precautions

1. Tax laws change from time to time and need to be checked.

2. A few of the stragegies we've discussed require professional counsel, but it's a good idea to discuss all of them with competent accountants, attorneys, trust officers, planned giving consultants, insurance agents, or investment planners.

3. There are sometimes limitations on the deductibility of gifts, so these need to be checked. General brochures and detailed illustrations of what various plans can do for you are available (see the resource center at the back of the book).

4. The ideas we have discussed are not difficult to implement, but you might have to review some illustrations about which are best for you according to your needs, goals, and situation.

5. Prayer should be a part of this process too.

Hospitals desperately need those who have the ability to smile and spend time with those who are suffering. The same is true of most facilities that care for the abused and suffering children (my wife's favorite cause) and adults in our society. The list goes on and on—it's as endless as the variety of individuals and talents at our command.

I believe many investors call me just because they need someone to talk to, and they are not alone. There are many people like that today. It would be wonderful if we could match our own abilities with those who need them so desperately.

Churches and local organizations can help everyone do just that. Senior citizens might also write to the American Association of Retired Persons. They operate a computer program that will match your interests and skills with volunteer efforts in your area. You don't need to be a member of AARP to use the service; you just need to be fifty or over. (Write them at: AARP Volunteer Talent Bank, 1909 K Street NW, Washington, DC 20049.)

My experiences helping people with money and observing them during retirement have proven one thing to me: Money has little to do with happiness. Spirituality and caring have everything to do with it.

Early in life we devote ourselves to making a living and raising our children. At times we all look forward to the day when job responsibilities will ease, the children will be raised, and we will have time for ourselves. But when that day comes, not being needed by our businesses and children can at times leave us feeling empty and lonely. By reaching out with faith, love, and caring for others, we can fill that void. That's real planned giving.

Case Studies

Following are three actual case studies I've done (the names have been changed), which may be helpful as comparisons if you are considering a planned giving program.

Mrs. John Jones
Widow, age 60

Seeks a safe income without management worries. Has a $25,000 cer-
tificate of deposit maturing. Would like to remember her church at her
death as efficiently as possible.

She calls her local planned giving contact or writes her stewardship office and asks for an illustration of the benefits of their pooled income
fund. The illustration shows:

1. Her contribution will pay an annual income based on the
   current interest rate of government bonds.
2. She will be entitled to a charitable deduction of $5,649.
3. She will incur no probate costs on the gift at death.
4. There will be no estate tax on the gift at death.

After comparing the proposal to a government securities mutual fund
proposed by her banker and broker, this is my analysis:

1. The mutual fund charges .6% yearly in management fees, which
   reduces the income paid. The pooled income fund doesn't.
   Extra annual income is $150 from this savings. Assuming Mrs.
   Jones lives to age 80, she will enjoy an extra $3,000 over her
   lifetime. The mutual fund charges a 4% commission to
   purchase. The pooled income fund doesn't. Savings is $1,000.
2. The charitable deduction saves Mrs. Jones $1,582 in her tax
   bracket.
3. Assuming 5% probate costs, the estate will save $1,250 at Mrs.
   Jones's death by using the pooled income fund.
4. Mrs. Jones's estate is under $600,000 so there is no estate tax
   savings. Otherwise, estate tax savings could be significant since
   the tax starts at 37%.
5. She could contribute to the pooled income fund. Use the
   $1,582 and $1,000 saved to purchase a zero-coupon bond for
   her new grandson's college expenses. At today's interest rates,
   the $2,582 will grow to approximately $13,000 by his
   eighteenth birthday. Earnings could be tax-free.

Financial summary: Mrs. Jones could enjoy $3,000 extra income over her lifetime, provide $13,000 for her grandson's education, and save approximately $1,250 in probate costs. Total financial benefit: $17,250.

Non-financial summary: Mrs. Jones could be relieved of management worries for the rest of her life and could leave a $25,000 gift to her church's work.

Disadvantages: The gift to the pooled income fund is irrevocable. Mrs. Jones should have other resources sufficient to meet her needs in an emergency.

Suggested action: Verify figures with tax counsel and proceed with a partial or full gift when assured that other assets are sufficient to meet her expenses.

(Case study prepared 1 June 1989)

Mr. and Mrs. John Smith
Ages 71 and 66

Invested $14,000 in a growth stock years ago. The stock has appreciated to $103,000. The stock doesn't pay a dividend. Mr. and Mrs. Smith would like retirement income, are concerned about the potential tax on their gain, and are concerned about a market decline which would reduce the value of their stock.

They call their local planned giving contact or write their stewardship office and ask for an illustration of the benefits of a pooled income fund (a charitable remainder trust could provide similar benefits). The illustration shows:

1. The pooled income fund can sell the stock and invest the total $103,000 into government bonds currently paying 9%. This will generate $9,270 per year extra income for Mr. and Mrs. Smith's lifetimes and saves $24,920 in tax on selling the stock.

2. They receive a charitable deduction of $20,805. This saves $5,825 in taxes in the 28% tax bracket.

3. They have not established trusts, so the estate can save $5,150 in probate, assuming 5% costs.

4. Their estate is under $600,000 so there is no estate tax savings. Otherwise, savings could be substantial since the tax begins at 37%.

After comparing the use of a pooled income fund to their current plans to hold the stock until death, this is my analysis:

1. We make the assumption that Mrs. Smith will survive Mr. Smith and will live to age 80. There would therefore be 14 years of income at $9,270 per year. Total income would approximate $130,000 over the rest of their lifetimes.

2. We assume no savings on capital gains since the government currently affords a "stepped up cost basis" on inherited property. This would effectively forgive the gains upon their death. This provision of the tax law changes occasionally. Any changes would affect them negatively in all probability.

3. The $5,825 saved by the charitable deduction could produce $25,000 to $30,000 of education funds for grandchildren if invested.

Financial summary: We feel comfortable that the income fund could provide about $130,000 of income over the rest of their lifetimes. We are certain tax savings could provide at least $25,000 for their grandchildren's education funds. We realize a government decision to eliminate or reduce the "stepped up cost basis" could cost us as much as $24,920. We believe we will save over $5,000 in probate costs by using the income fund. We therefore reasonably assume a total financial benefit of approximately $160,000, which could be as much as $24,920 higher if the government affects us negatively. Any declines in the value of the stock (which is one of our assumptions) would add to the merits of converting to the income fund.

Non-financial summary: Mr. and Mrs. Smith can be relieved of concern about the market fluctuations of their stock and can leave a gift of $103,000 to their church.

Disadvantages: The gift to the pooled income fund is irrevocable, although this is of less concern since they do not plan to sell the stock anyway. But it could be important in a financial emergency. Other resources should be sufficient to meet any needs. Any appreciation in the stock donated will be lost for heirs. The pooled income fund will provide taxable income, perhaps a tax disadvantage.

Suggested action: Verify all figures with tax counsel and proceed with all or a part of the stock, assuming they are confident their remaining assets will meet their needs.

(Case study prepared 15 April 1989)

Mr. and Mrs. Jack Brown
Ages 62 and 60

Mrs. and Mrs. Brown have a $10,000 investment maturing. They have been reinvesting the income since they don't currently need it. There is a possibility they could need it in an emergency or if inflation worsens. They are in the 28% tax bracket and are concerned about tax management. They desire to leave this account to their church if they do not need it during their lifetimes. They are fairly sure they won't, but aren't totally certain.

They consider investing in an annuity and naming the church as beneficiary. They contact their local planned giving officer and have him coordinate the proposals from their investment broker, insurance agent, and possibly from their church insurance company. From this we make the following assessment:

1. The chosen annuity pays the same 9% rate as the taxable investments they are considering.

2. We make the assumption that Mrs. Brown will survive Mr. Brown and live to age 80.

3. Mrs. Brown has adequate income during her lifetime and doesn't need to access the interest after all (not unusual in my experiences as an investment counselor).

My analysis, after comparing the annuity to the taxable investment.

1. Each earns 9% on average per year. The annuity accumulates without tax but there is tax on the interest paid by the taxable investment.

2. Both accumulate interest each year and earn an average of 9% until Mrs. Brown's death at age 80. Proposals show the annuity would accumulate to $56,044. The taxable account would accumulate to $35,104.

3. There is no probate on the annuity at Mrs. Brown's death. This saves $2,802 in expense at her death.

Summary: The annuity allows the Browns to give over $20,000 more to their church since income taxes are essentially forgiven when the church receives the money. They have maintained control of their money during their lifetimes. Should the need arise, they could change the beneficiary to their children by simply writing the annuity company. There are no management worries while the annuity accumulates. There is no immediate income tax deduction since they maintain control of the money.

Suggested action: Search for a company with the credentials described in this book. Investing in an annuity can be accomplished in about fifteen minutes once the annuity is chosen.

(Case study prepared 12 April 1989)

12

Fundamentals of Estate Planning

The measure of a man's value is the degree to which he has made a difference in the lives of those he has touched.

Jackie A. Strange

YOU ONLY HAVE TO READ a few pages of the Bible, fifteen chapters of Genesis to be exact, to discover the passion men and women have always had to leave an earthly heritage and to see their worldly goods passed on to their children. As you read of Abraham's concerns in Genesis 15, notice that God cared about Abraham's wishes and made ample provision for them. But also notice that God was more concerned that Abraham pass on his spiritual heritage to future generations. The priorities evident in this passage should be prayerfully considered by any Christian before making estate plans.

Goals of Estate Planning

Estate planning accomplishes three things, all having to do with your material possessions. First, it assures that your assets will be dispersed as you want them to be—when and to whom. Second, it assures that they are dispensed with a minimum of bother and administrative expense. Third, it assures that they are dispensed with a minimum amount paid in federal estate taxes.

Estate planning is a formidable sounding phrase and many view it as a very complex process. For the vast majority of people it is not.

The Right Way . . . the Wrong Way

Your assets will be distributed one of two ways: either as you direct or as the government dictates. (If you have any reticence at all about entering estate planning, I strongly urge you to consider the way the government handles money!) Fortunately, the government will only dominate the picture if you fail to prepare a will or other legal vehicle to designate your desires. Failure to do this means "dying intestate,"

291

which means that a local judge will divide your assets according to state law. This varies from state to state, but usually gives half to the surviving spouse and divides the remaining half among your children. That can be very unfair if your spouse is on a fixed income and your children are grown, working, and doing well. Don't let it happen. (Things get even more complicated when divorce or second marriages and stepchildren enter the picture.)

Your assets will be distributed one of two ways: either as you direct or as the government dictates.

Your Will

The easiest way to avoid problems is to prepare a will. This usually takes an hour or two at an attorney's office and is relatively inexpensive. Choose a lawyer who specializes in or is knowledgeable about the subject. (I can assure you all are not.) If your estate will need investment decisions made, I might prefer a trust department above most attorneys.

If you have any reticence about estate planning, I strongly urge you to consider the way the government handles money!

In drawing up a will you simply indicate who should get what and name a "personal representative," often called an executor, to handle the details after your death. This can be a relative, friend, attorney, or bank trust department. Wills do require that your estate go before a probate judge after you die, but a will simplifies the process. The judge merely assures that your assets are allocated as you stipulated and that your bills and taxes are paid. Probate can be expensive, however, since some states require that an attorney or the trust department's attorney accompany your estate to court along with the executor, and both should be paid for their time from your estate.

Controlling Costs

Perhaps you have heard horror stories about estates being decimated by attorney fees and other expenses. These are often exaggerated, but they do prove a point. You will not be around to watch over your assets, and your heirs will have no idea what you and your attorney discussed regarding compensation. For this reason, it's a good idea to have a written estimate attached to your will to prevent any misunderstandings. This should be a good-faith estimate of the total cost for handling your estate. It should allow for inflation, changes in the complexity of your affairs, increases in your estate, and increases in the number of people involved in the inheritance.

Handling an estate does take time, so expect to compensate your attorney. Ask your attorney to let you know up front about the costs. If he or she is offended by this request, I suggest you find another attorney. Many even have printed fee schedules prepared in advance.

293

Avoiding Probate

Some assets do not need to go through the probate process. I mentioned earlier that insurance contracts and annuities that have a named beneficiary do not. Your personal representative simply attaches a certified copy of a death certificate to the policy, sends it to the company, and they send the proceeds to the heirs. The same is true with qualified plans (such as IRAs) where you've named a beneficiary. These assets normally pass to the named beneficiary even if your will says to leave everything you own to another person—an important point to be aware of.

Assets held in joint name, such as certificates of deposit or securities, do not need to go through probate. The surviving owner gives a copy of the death certificate, and sometimes a form called an "Affidavit of Domicile" (according to what the particular state requires), to your bank or broker and it's quickly done. Banks also allow you to put a child's name on a certificate so it avoids probate. Don't do that with securities, however, unless you've discussed it with an expert. This is also true for your home and other assets. Many people put a child's name on assets to simplify estate matters and end up creating problems in other areas. For example, it can diminish the over-age-55 tax exemption for selling your home at a profit (your child may be under 55 and therefore not qualified). Also, your will cannot direct assets that are held jointly. They go to the joint owner.

Trusts

Assets may also bypass probate if you have used a trust. Trusts are often viewed as complicated and/or expensive and consequently are overlooked by many who could really benefit from them. While they can be complicated, there are some relatively simple ones that serve the needs of most people. Trusts do one or a combination of three things: provide expert control of assets, reduce probate costs, and/or reduce federal estate taxes.

Trusts are overlooked by many who could really benefit from them.

The Language of Trusts

Trusts have their own language. A "trustor" is the person creating the trust. A "trustee" is the person, charity, or bank who will manage the trust. The "beneficiary" is the person who receives the benefits of the trust at the death of the trustor or at a time he or she has designated.

Testamentary Trusts

A "testamentary trust" is so named because it is created by your last will and testament. It is usually used to provide control of assets. For example, my will could say, "I leave all my assets to my son," who is my only heir, if my wife and I die together in an accident. But my son is only two years old. I wouldn't care to have him manage my estate, even if the law would allow it. So I could have my will say, "I leave all my assets to a trust for my son," stipulating that a friend, relative, or bank trust department manage the money. In addition, I could have the trust say, "I give my son control of the money when he turns twenty-five" or any other age I think is appropriate. Without being there, I have controlled the way and the time my son gets my estate.

A testamentary trust must go through probate since it is created through your will, so it doesn't eliminate probate expense. It may save on estate taxes if needed and if it is prepared properly.

The Living Trust

Some trusts provide benefits for the trustor as long as he or she is alive; many of my clients are both the trustor and the trustee. In other words, they manage their own affairs for their own benefit as long as they live. Then their heirs enjoy the benefits of the trust when it comes time to pass on the assets.

An "inter vivos" or "living trust" is so named because the trust is for the living. These often are used to avoid the expense and delays of probate, although they can have other significant benefits, such as providing professional management of your estate for your heirs. You simply have an attorney create a trust to hold your assets; you may be the trustee and manage the assets, and you get all the income and gains from the trust. However, your assets do not have to go through probate at your death since the trust technically owns them, not you. Your personal representative simply provides a death certificate and the assets are distributed according to the directions of the trust.

Trusts are normally revocable (meaning you can cancel them or change them at any time) and you can change the trustee and beneficiaries if you choose. For example, should you become disabled you can name a friend or bank to be the trustee and manage your assets.

I have found that some attorneys are not totally objective about the benefits of living trusts. Sitting before an attorney and asking about a living trust is like sitting in front of a broker and asking for a substantial discount on your commissions. Essentially you are asking the attorneys how to minimize their fees in getting your assets to your heirs. I have had attorneys tell my clients there was no need to spend $1,000 for such a trust and then, when asked, turn around and estimate a $20,000 fee for guiding that same estate through probate. The benefits of the trust may have eluded the attorney but they were instantly apparent to my clients.

Most people who have money enough to need financial counselors and planned giving officers would benefit from a trust. For further information I suggest you go to your local library and read two articles: *Forbes*, 26 December 1988 (page 126); and *The Wall Street Journal*, 4 February 1987 (page 1, section 2).

If you do create a trust, be sure to put all your assets in the name of the trust. Simply creating a trust, without re-registering the securities or other assets involved, can leave you exposed to probate, accomplishing nothing.

Estate Taxation

Generally, your estate will be taxed on any assets worth $600,000 or more (this number tends to change quite a bit as different politicians control Washington, so check it from time to time). This figure includes all your assets, whether in your name or held jointly, as well as such things as life insurance proceeds. The tax on assets above $600,000 begins at 37% and peaks at 55%. You can leave amounts larger than that without tax to one of two parties—spouses and churches or charities. They can usually receive any amount without estate taxes.

It is very important that married couples with assets potentially subject to tax do their estate planning before the death of the first spouse. As I said, you can leave any amount to a spouse without tax, but the surviving spouse's estate can be hurt severely when he or she dies. The remaining spouse has no one (other than a charity or church) who can benefit from an unlimited deduction. This example should illustrate the point.

Mr. Jones has a net worth of $1,000,000. He has a simple reciprocal will (I call this the "I love you, honey" will) that leaves everything to Mrs. Jones. When he dies, the $1,000,000 goes to her without tax. BUT, Mrs. Jones's will says to leave her assets to their only son (who is not a spouse or church/charity). Her $1,000,000 estate is reduced by the $600,000 exemption and the remaining $400,000 is taxed. That tax today is over $150,000.

The "A & B" Trust

This tax could have been avoided if Mr. Jones had established an "A & B" trust. It's called that because he divides his assets into "part A" and "part B." When divided this way, "part A" goes to Mrs. Jones without restriction, while "part B" remains in a trust that will pay her income for the rest of her life, but is structured to pay anything remaining to their son at her death. Since the money (not the income) is going to their son, it is not Mrs. Jones's and therefore not included in her estate at her death. Assuming "part A" and "part B" were split evenly, at her death Mrs. Jones has $500,000 in her name; this can pass tax-free to their son, since it's less than $600,000. The trust can pass tax-free too, so the entire $1,000,000 can be passed without tax. A simple trust usually costs about $1,000 to set up (at least that is the case in Tampa) and saves estate taxes—in our example that was $150,000. Not a bad investment.

Couples can normally pass up to $1,200,000 to children without taxes if they plan properly before the death of the first spouse. The use of "irrevocable insurance trusts," "charitable remainder trusts," and "grantor retained income trusts" often allow even more. Ask your financial counselor or planner about these. The limit is usually $600,000 after the death of the first spouse, so make your estate plans early enough to avoid this.

Other Tax Strategies

If you wish to leave more than these amounts to your heirs, without being subject to taxes, there are two other avenues you can take. First, each person can give up to $10,000 each year to anyone (and $10,000 to as many people as they choose) without gift tax (which is now the same as estate tax). Couples could therefore give up to $20,000 each year ($10,000 apiece) to any children or grandchildren and remove those amounts from their taxable estates. Using this technique, surprising amounts can be removed, tax-free, from your estate over the years. (Congress subjects this to scrutiny from time to time but hasn't changed it yet since so few people use it.)

Second, I said earlier that you can normally leave any amount you choose to church or charity without estate tax. For example, assume Mr. Jones did not create the "A & B" trust and left the entire $1,000,000 to Mrs. Jones. She could leave $600,000 to their son without tax and the remaining $400,000 to her church and charities without any tax. I would hope charitable intent is the motivating factor, of course, but the tax advantages do make it more attractive (which is why Congress allows it in the first place).

Some states impose their own estate tax and others, like Florida, don't. In this case, I have clients who divide their time each year between two states who can benefit by making Florida their legal residence. If you have this option, examine your alternatives. Then be sure to update your wills and trusts according to the laws of the state where you make your legal residence.

As you read my advice in this section, some of you may question the matter of avoiding taxes on such large estates. Certainly there *is* a matter of ethics involved in how much the law allows us to pass from generation to generation. But as I've stated before, I'm not here to draw lines—only to help you draw your own. Again I say, always examine your own motives, and question whether the largest estate is the best thing for your children.

Guardianship for Children

Some people don't worry about estate planning because they aren't overly concerned about what their heirs will do with their money after they're gone. However, estate planning becomes critical for those with young children. Essentially the government considers your children a part of your estate if you haven't planned for them. Every young family should have a will if for no other reason than to establish guardianship for their children. (A guardian essentially becomes a substitute parent.) And careful thought should be given to the persons named as potential guardians. Consider their stability, economic circumstances, religious beliefs, and so forth. Remember, if something should happen to you, these are the individuals who will be raising your children. Not a matter to be taken lightly.

Every young family should have a will.

Many people automatically name relatives, but this is not always the best course. When my wife and I chose our son's godparents to be his potential guardians, we didn't have any younger relatives with stable family situations. So we chose this couple who are close to our ages, go to our church, and have similar interests. Should anything happen to us, the trust we established for our son will immediately dispense an amount that will allow them to fix a room for him in their home, and will later provide for his education and other reasonable expenses. He gets control of the trust when he turns thirty-five. We did the planning for our son's benefit, but it also gives us peace of mind.

Measure the Heart

In many ways, the advice I give about estate planning and attorneys/trust departments is comparable to what I've said about investment planning and brokers/planners. A broker who does not have your best interests at heart is a horrible source of investment advice. An attorney without your best interests at heart is a horrible source of estate planning advice. Also, experience and specialization can be a crucial factor. Some well-intentioned attorneys do not know any more about estate planning than some well-intentioned young brokers know about investments. In fact, many attorneys receive no estate planning education while in law school.

Some attorneys advertise "cheap" and offer near complimentary will preparation, only to present an expensive bill for the free lunch after they've probated your estate. Avoid them as you would the broker/planner who never charges a fee or commission. I would discourage allowing items that avoid probate, such as IRAs and annuities, to be put in the "probated estate"

301

for purposes of attorney's fees. A small fee might be appropriate for handling them, but some of these fees seem excessive since probate is not necessary.

Check the Performance

You can buy a mutual fund through a broker and benefit from the expertise and convenience or you can do it yourself and save the commission. You can use a trust department's expertise and convenience or you can manage your own trust and save the fee. I've had clients pay thousands of dollars to have trust departments do nothing more than provide custody for securities and collect income (the same things all investment firms do for nothing). This doesn't make much sense. But trust departments are worth their fees if they manage and/or oversee your assets properly. Sizable trust departments often operate their own investment funds with actual performance numbers available—often very good ones. Ask to see them and compare them to better mutual funds and money managers. Avoid using a trust department just because "good old Harry, the local trust department contact" is always at the club along with all the brokers in town. Use him only if his money management skills are proven and his service is valuable.

Otherwise, consider putting your assets with some proven mutual funds or money managers and naming yourself or a friend with business acumen as your trustee. Name a bank as "successor trustee" to take over in case the trustee dies or doesn't wish to continue watching over the mutual funds or money managers. Far too many people accept inferior investment performance simply for trust services. You want both.

Apply the same criteria you would when "hiring" a broker. Take a hard look at their experience and track record. Trust departments are conservative and promise to "preserve" your estate. That often means they won't do anything to lose your money . . . or to make you any either. The performance of my son's trust may well be more important than the performance of my own investment portfolio, so I have planned to assure that it is well-managed. You should do the same.

Summary

No matter what the size of their estate, I always advise my clients to have an attorney prepare a will for them. It should name a guardian for any minor children and establish a trust to manage assets until the children reach an age you think is appropriate for them to gain control. The trust should name a bank trust department or an individual you respect to manage the assets (there are such individuals called "personal trust officers" too). I also encourage my clients to remember churches and charities they care about along with their heirs.

Ask your attorney to estimate any expenses for getting the estate through the probate process and compare that to the expenses of a living trust. If the costs are less and the anticipated administrative matters are reduced through the latter, you should probably prepare a living trust.

Estates projected to be subject to federal estate tax might consider trusts and gifting programs to children and churches or charities to minimize those taxes. At the time of this writing, these estates are those above $600,000. Have your attorney or financial planner monitor any changes in that number.

Consider establishing trusts to manage assets for anyone (whether minor or not) who may not manage the money properly. Seriously evaluate whether all your heirs can handle money. Institutions such as your local bank trust department are convenient. Be sure they have proven money management skills if you need them. Assuming they do not have a proven record of managing money, ask them to provide custody for your securities and find outside money managers or mutual funds who do have proven records. Your heirs may live with these decisions for a long time, so be sure they are solidly thought out.

Some Disclaimers Are Appropriate

First, estate planning is a very dangerous area to study and attempt yourself. This chapter only seeks to point out areas you might need to address, not to provide specific advice. I am not an attorney, but have adapted this chapter from writings by attorneys I respect. (I'm particularly grateful to Harold Harkins, attorney and trust officer in Tampa, and to Donald Wells of the Commerce National Trust Division in Lexington, Kentucky.)

Second, estate planning laws vary from state to state, and tax law is complicated and changes rapidly. Seek the assistance of an attorney or trust department whose head and heart measure up in expertise, empathy, and ethical standards.

13

Money Is Not Enough

Over the years I've been convinced that nothing exists except God. There is no other reality.

Sir John M. Templeton

AFTER THE STOCK MARKET CRASH of October 1987 the popular television show "Wall Street Week" canceled its regular guest and called on John Templeton and two other pillars of Wall Street to address what they knew was an anxious audience. In his typically quiet manner, Mr. Templeton reassured the viewers by telling them to maintain faith. His spiritual foundation surely played an essential role in his assertion that a stock market crash would not be the end of the world.

Perspective such as this prompted one of my friends to tell me recently that he hates two things about Mr. Templeton . . . that he's always realistically optimistic . . . and that he's always right in the long run!

I can think of no higher tribute, and I can think of no better approach for an investor in our modern world. Today's financial community is a major source of stress, confusion, and turmoil for many of us, including Christians. Yet it doesn't need to be if we truly understand the real power of Christianity.

The central ethic of Christianity is love, and anyone who pursues a deeper understanding of this often begins with Saint Paul's famous words in the thirteenth chapter of 1 Corinthians—words most people, no matter what they believe, are familiar with.

> Love is patient and kind; it is not jealous or conceited or proud; love is not ill-mannered or selfish or irritable; love does not keep a record of wrongs; love is not happy with evil, but is happy with the truth. Love never gives up; and its faith, hope, and patience never fail. Love is eternal.

As I've searched a multitude of books and reports written by and about pillars of Wall Street during the past years, I have become convinced that a perspective based on these words could do much to solve the concerns expressed about the Street recently. My studies have also convinced me that few people on the Street have applied these words with greater sincerity and success than John Templeton, founder of the Templeton Mutual Funds and most recently one of the first four inductees into "Wall Street Week's" Hall of Fame. (Despite a low-risk management style, the Templeton Growth Fund has apparently been the most rewarding of any in the world over its 35 years of existence.)

Mr. Templeton has three qualities that have served him well as an investor, says John Schroeder, respected chairman of the Axe-Houghton Funds. Mr. Templeton is brilliant, has the courage to act on his convictions, and "he's a spiritual man, which gives him stability and a long range sense of purpose and hope." It's enlightening to compare that description to the qualities listed by Saint Paul.

In a financial world exhibiting an increasing desire for short-term rewards, John Templeton holds his investments an average of five to six years. While many Wall Street regulars pursue wealth in every and any conceivable way, he avoids many investments that support the production of products that might be harmful to humanity or are speculative in nature. He strongly promotes the merits of giving, and he faithfully gives a double tithe to his church. Also, anyone who has ever visited Mr. Templeton in his office is immediately struck by the contrast between the serenity his quiet demeanor has created for his associates and the frenzied traders in the turmoil of the major exchanges, options floors, and commodities pits.

Mr. Templeton is a master of understatement. While others on Wall Street easily make promises and claims, he simply says, "We'll do the best we can for you" to those who entrust their money to his care. And while the pursuit of money is all-encompassing for many on our Street, John Templeton has devoted considerable time and effort over the years to humbly pursuing and sharing the will of God. He freely admits his mistakes—mistakes every investor must make over the years. But he does not dwell on them. He simply learns from them and proceeds in a wiser fashion. His understanding of the true value of money and his spiritual balance produce a very evident inner peace and a joy for all that life has to offer. While professionals and philosophies change frequently on Wall Street, Mr. Templeton and his humble approaches seem eternal in nature.[1]

John Templeton is living proof that the Christian ethic of love offers a solution to the financial community—and the world—as the twentieth century draws to a close. But in doing so, this ethic also asks some tough questions and demands some honest self-examination.

The Prescription of Love

Earlier I quoted John Wesley, who said, "Make all you can, save all you can, and give all you can." Clearly Wesley understood how important making money is, but he certainly was not preaching a theology of greed. His earliest followers were known to work extra hours just so they could give more to others.

One of the saddest questions I hear from time to time is, "If I have what I need, why bother to do more?" Obviously those who ask this can't see beyond themselves. The world is filled with people who have great needs,

---

1 The author would like readers to know that the comments made about John Templeton were written after he had graciously endorsed this book. Since his endorsement, there have been many articles and books published about Mr. Templeton's works and philosophies that are so pertinent to this subject that I have tried to focus them into these few paragraphs.

immediate needs—like their next meal or a roof over their heads.

Money is not a luxury nor a statement of who we are; it is a resource. A resource that must be placed firmly at the feet of God. And once that is done, it is a resource that can daily shape our world for the better.

Our responsible approach to borrowing can assure that our children will not be overburdened with interest on our national debt and will keep money available for higher priority investing. Our daily earning can do much more than just provide for our own security and satisfaction; it can support churches, children's homes, programs for the poor, hospitals, and schools. Our savings can do more than just provide financial security for ourselves and our loved ones; they can also benefit our neighbor. Invested wisely and ethically they can help clean our rivers and air, provide housing, generate dignified jobs, and offer necessities to the less fortunate, to young families, and to the elderly. Our gifts can do more than save us taxes; through tithes and planned giving we can support churches, schools, and worthy charities for decades to come. Our responsible, ethical actions today can help assure that our children will live in a prosperous but moral, caring world tomorrow. It's a simple matter of priorities.

Yet I believe we can also prosper today if we maintain our perspective and discipline. Economies tend to move from depression periods, like the 1930s, when there is too little money around, through periods of stable business conditions when there is an appropriate amount of money around, to inflationary periods, like the late 1970s, when there is too much money around. A balanced investment portfolio containing high-quality bonds, utility stocks, and insurance contracts provides protection during slow economies; money market investments and real estate prosper during inflationary periods; and high-quality stocks shine during periods of stability. Rather than guessing at the future, the creation of a diversified portfolio plans for any future.

Spreading money prudently can provide a more peaceful world too. Making the resources of wealth available for all the truly productive areas of society that require financing helps avoid the chaos that develops when one sector of the financial community attracts too much money. For example, too much money chased oil during the 1970s, causing a boom-bust scenario that closed banks and devastated real estate in the oil belt. Too much money chased real estate during the same period, resulting in failed mortgages that hurt many banks, while limited partnerships hurt individual investors. It might be argued that the explosion of credit card and consumer loan advertisements during the late 1980s resulted from a flight of money to the banks after the stock market crash. A stable allocation of money helps assure a stable society.

Maintaining a long-term perspective with our stock and bond money minimizes the short-term, massive movement of money that so disrupts our public markets. Avoiding stock market trading and mutual funds that excessively trade and "allocate" money in a different way each month can provide more stability for the stock market. This stability can then assure that Americans will once again be ready to finance the growing companies that create needed jobs and keep us competitive in a rapidly changing world. Holding bonds until they mature helps minimize interest rate swings and can make banks and investors more willing to commit to the longer term financing so critical to our prosperity. And refusing to become involved in options and futures, either individually or through mutual funds, turns our attention from speculating against our neighbors to producing for them.

A disciplined allocation of gifts and investment monies to their highest possible uses can be both service to humanity and worship of God.

The Christian Economic Perspective in a Modern World

It's no secret that a selective reading of Christian guidance can create havoc. Remember the medieval crusaders who killed and plundered in the name of God? We can justify becoming a modern version of a robber baron—engaged in massive, self-centered accumulation—by selectively embracing certain stewardship concepts. Even the magnificent parable of the talents—where stewards multiplied their master's wealth in creative ways—can be dangerous if we ignore the sobering parable of the fool who built bigger barns with no regard for neighbor or God. That's why, in taking Wesley's admonition about finances, it's vital that we not try to adapt suggestions one and two without suggestion three. But if we strike a balance of all three—ethical earning, ethical investing, and generous giving—we can provide real answers for a troubled world. Then money becomes more than an end in itself; it becomes a means for solving some of the world's problems.

A firm embracing of the parable of the talents and the parable of the fool is the answer to the "question for the future" asked in the opening pages of this book.

Critics of capitalism have long believed that our free economic system cannot survive humanity's self-interested greed. They maintain that capitalism can dramatically produce wealth but can't distribute it equitably. The government must place constraints and distribute the wealth, they say. But recent events in Eastern Europe are proving that laws and economic shackles cannot be as effective as economic freedom and individual initiative constrained by ethical guidelines. I believe they are discovering that there is nothing ideal about having the government equitably distribute less than people need. Men and women were created for so much more than that—the promised land of milk and honey if you will.

Yet we in America must realize that the founders of our nation never meant for it to be based solely on "free enterprise." That was simply part of the freedom guaranteed to each individual. Our coinage says "In God We Trust," and our Pledge of Allegiance affirms that we are to be "one nation under God." Underlying everything is an Infinite source of respect for the common good.

Through the decades our populace has often wavered in its dedication to ethical ideals. Recently this has become even more evident with the escalation of greed and excessive self-interested dealings in banking institutions, on Wall Street, in government appropriations, and even in television ministries. With the great freedoms we have inherited, it also seems we have inherited great opportunity to repeatedly demonstrate that men and women need a deep understanding of the Absolute if they are to keep things in proper perspective. Market participants and governments far too often change the definitions of "right," "prudent," and "responsible."

So we encounter a world that has limited expectations of government but a fear of the free market—a world that seeks a solid foundation on which to build a just prosperity. Our proposal here is that the solution lies in a return to the Christian notion of charity and an "ethical market," where one neighbor cares for another neighbor through the free expression of love.

I said at the beginning of this book that I do not pretend to know whether God prefers government to control the wealth or free markets to control it. I reaffirm that here. But our concept of a 10% tithe and charity combined with a 10% savings rate flowing to an "ethical market" places great hope in our church members combined with limited hope in our government leaders.

While I acknowledge the legitimate, indeed critical, role of government in many endeavors, I am less optimistic about government than are many of my friends, and for three very practical reasons.

First, recent elections cause me to wonder if we can elect leaders who agree that heavier taxes are required. In other words, will modern America vote to tax itself more heavily? And while it's not unusual for politicians to promise "no new taxes" but seek them indirectly, this creates an ethical environment no responsible person could support. Our country desperately needs higher ethical leadership from Washington and our statehouses.

Second, I am uncertain whether taxes that are collected will be used in the highest moral sense. It often seems the benefits of tax dollars are increasingly influenced by monied lobbyists rather than the homeless and hungry. Tax dollars too often assure a hold on power, not a home for the powerless.

Third, we pay a large overhead bill for social programs operated by the government. Appropriations must be evaluated on the basis of how much goes to the needy and how much goes to government staffers.

Until we reform the goals of the "free market" AND the priorities of government, I'll place the bulk of my faith in love. Like all economic approaches, this is more than a bit idealistic. But I believe it's the one the Master suggested—and I pray to God it's one that can still find acceptance in America.

In the financial world, let us share the example of those like John Templeton who have maintained their perspective of love during a decade of financial folly. In the spiritual world, let us show them a faith that is capable and ready to play a major role in our rededication to that ethic which encourages fair play between neighbors. I'm convinced it could light the way to a more effective and responsible capitalism for the 1990s throughout the world.

Our churches are filled with Christians who have available to them financial insights that have helped generations of Americans survive depression and inflation; droughts, floods, tornadoes, and dust bowls; and the failures of government and economic systems. God's still, small voice has always counseled diligence, thrift, compassion, and truly beneficial work, and that is where our industry and society will find the answers they so desperately seek.

Then we will no longer need to study Japanese methods. We will no longer need to borrow their money. We will turn a good economy into an even stronger, more broadly beneficial one. Then we will be spared the anxicty over troubled governmental devices like the Social Security Trust Fund, the FSLIC Insurance Fund, misdirected budget appropriations, lax securities regulation, enormous budget deficits, and cutbacks in social programs. The resources for our security and the security of those around us lie in individual responsibility . . . but allocated by the love of God for the common good.

The Christian ethic of love has always held the answer to materialism, greed, and political turmoil. And when the E. F. Huttons are silenced, the voice of God can be heard, telling us to use our resources in ways that are productive for the good of all creation.

315

A Personal Reflection

By now it is no secret to you that the teachings of the Christian faith have radically but-oh-so-positively in-fluenced my view of the financial world. Though I am only a beginning student of God's economic ways, those teachings have already guided me through several stages. First came the breaking open of the protective cocoon I had spun for myself by attending church and giving regularly. Like the Pharisee praying in the temple, I needed to understand that wasn't enough. I was giving a relatively small amount of my time and money, and God wanted it all. I found that even a tith-ing Christian could not make peace with his money when the other 90% was engaged in purely self-serving purposes.

Learning to understand that any blessings I have are by the grace of God was the second stage. Even the Protestant work ethic that I value so highly didn't bring these blessings. There are talented, hardworking people throughout the world who do not enjoy the blessings most Americans do. Our individual prosperity is de-pendent upon proper institutional arrangements as well as our individual efforts. (The Israelites worked very hard in Egypt, but the institutional arrangements didn't allow them to prosper as slaves.) This was a humbling lesson for me. But understanding that simple fact made the offering of thanksgiving to God and the giving of tithes and charity more meaningful. And it made me care more about the corporate, social, and governmental structures of the world.

The third stage encouraged me to be a good steward of these blessings and to search for ways to practice what I said I believed within the structures that do exist. It's wonderful to talk about "being a good steward of God's money," but it's incredibly important to find

316

out exactly what that means and how it can be accomplished. Hollow phrases do not provide jobs, low-income housing, or a clean environment, nor do they finance our churches and charities in the future.

And the fourth stage, I'm just beginning to understand, is the knowledge that my finances are relatively insignificant in the total picture of faith. Ethical investments and responsible use of possessions are an integral part of, but in no way substitute for, spirituality itself. Our real efforts must be directed toward developing the world spiritually, not materially or financially. Christian economists and investment bankers may solve short-term concerns, but only by living out the Word of God in the fullest sense will we solve the long-term ones. Hearts need to be born into a new life. This is the ultimate answer to the broader and seemingly overwhelming problems such as single-parent families, substance abuse, crime, and racism.

And I have a deep, growing suspicion that my future lessons will very likely reflect Martin Luther's observation that

> All who call upon God earnestly and in true faith will surely be heard and receive according to their petition; though perhaps not at the very hour and time, nor in the measure of their petition, nor exactly what they pray for, yet they will receive something much better, greater, and more glorious.

Unless I'm missing the point, I believe that the blessings I seek and give praise for are likely to be spiritual as often as financial. And this means that I cannot close this book on the merits of ethical investing and planned giving without cautioning you that the life of faith is not a meal ticket or a free ride. Bad things do happen to good people. The cross is an everlasting symbol of the peaks and valleys of any Christian life. The

God of faith simply promises peace and hope as we travel a world filled with pain, hurt, and disappointment.

No matter how ethical you are in your investing patterns, you will be subject to difficult economic periods along with the rest of the world. God didn't tell Joseph how to avoid the seven lean years. God simply told him to use the seven prosperous ones to prepare for them and then left it to Joseph to figure out how this guidance might help him accomplish that. I hope that's what we've started to do here in a much different world.

True Christian Financial Planning

Many books end with an appendix that readers seldom look at. This one ends with what I call a "resource center," and it is the most important part of the book. I emphatically ask that you explore it. There you will be introduced to the true authors of this book: dedicated churchpeople, charities, credit unions, banks, money managers, and others who have labored behind the headlines for years, attempting to route money to worthwhile causes and trying to address many ethical concerns of the financial world. I'm sure there are others who do equally fine work; these are simply the ones I'm aware of. Please review these carefully and thoughtfully, and understand that this book will do very little for you if you simply agree with its principles. Christian blueprints for building a better world are of little value unless we use them.

As you explore these financial tools and plans, relate your use of the resource of money to your use of the resources of time and talent. Consciously or subconsciously, we all fall somewhere on the spectrum from barely attending to God's work to selfless service. Some simply attend church on Christmas and Easter or for deaths and baptisms; some attend occasionally; some attend each Sunday and serve God daily in their secular vocations; some serve full-time in the more formal ministry, either in the pulpit or as Mother Teresa does in the streets of Calcutta. Financially, some make the barest donations; some contribute small weekly gifts; some give 10% or more, making sure that the other 90% is used in ways that honor the Christian ethic; and a few selflessly give their wealth to any who might need it.

Ethical investing and planned giving balance our interests with the interests of others. Neither attempts to detract from, nor substitute for, selfless giving, which is the greatest financial activity any Christian can experience. Each simply recognizes that we don't have to give all our money away to be good stewards, any more than we have to attend to the homeless of Calcutta to make good use of our time and talents. Each simply avoids self-centered accumulation.

Every day of your life you make decisions about how you earn money, how you invest money, how other people use your money, how you use other people's money, and how you give money. The ethical choices are complex and numerous enough to fill many books. But they are also amazingly simple if you examine each in the light of the ethic of love: how do they reflect love of God, love of neighbor, and love of yourself. All the teachings of faith hang on these three, and our long and glorious Christian heritage assures that they will provide the answers we need.

I wish you much success in finding the right combination of earning, investing, and giving for your small, but very important part in God's plan. May you find peace with the decisions you make throughout your financial and spiritual journey. Yet may God, in the form of a gentle discomfort, encourage each of you to continue a diligent search for the answers that will make the world a more prosperous and peaceful place for all.

Two thousand years ago a very special Man walked this earth. He said startling things that rocked the establishment—like "the first shall be last"—because he knew things aren't always what they seem. He looked deeper than first impressions and challenged conventional wisdom. He was a king who spent his days serving others. Many of his ancestors possessed great wealth, yet he was born in a stable and never owned a home. He bypassed many rich and prominent people who found it impossible to soften their hearts; he broke bread with social outcasts and poverty-stricken widows who yearned for the ways of God. And those who passionately worship him over twenty centuries later show forever the value money really plays in determining a person's "worth."

Never has the world needed him more than it does today, and he is still here. He is here when you care for Creation. He is here when you give to the destitute. He is here when you finance a home for a young family. He is here when you provide jobs for the unemployed. He is here when you sustain a church, educate a youth, or endow a charity.

He is here when you love.

Estate and Planned Giving Resources

The following members of the **National Council of Church's Estate and Financial Planning Forum** invite your inquiries about investment vehicles and planning services offered.[1]

American Baptist Foundation
P.O. Box 851
Valley Forge, PA 19482-0851
(They also have an Office of Social and Ethical Responsibility that invites inquiries at the same address.)

Christian Church Foundation
(Disciples of Christ)
James R. Reed, President
222 South Downey Avenue
P.O. Box 1986
Indianapolis, IN 46206

The Episcopal Church
Frederick Osborn
815 Second Avenue
New York, NY 10017

Presbyterian Church (USA) Foundation
200 East Twelfth Street
Jeffersonville, IN 47130

Reformed Church in America
Office of Gift Planning
1790 Grand Boulevard
Schenectady, NY 12309

United Church of Christ
Planned Giving Program
475 Riverside Drive
New York, NY 10115

The following members of the **board of the Christian Stewardship Association** invite your inquiries about investment vehicles and planning services offered.

Africa Inland Mission
John A. Barney
Director of Stewardship
P.O. Box 178
Pearl River, NY 10965

Back to the Bible
Stewardship Department
P.O. Box 82808
Lincoln, NE 68501

---

1 All listings are for information purposes only; inclusion does not necessarily imply an endorsement of this book.

Baptist General Conference
Development Division
2002 S. Arlington Heights Road
Arlington Heights, IL 60005

Christian and Missionary Alliance
Dr. Stanley Bjornson
15000 Shell Point Boulevard
Fort Meyers, FL 33908

Church of God
Department of Stewardship
P.O. Box 2430
Cleveland, TN 37320

Compassion International
Russ Reid
P.O. Box 7000
Colorado Springs, CO 80933

Evangelical Free Church of America
Gene Jones
1515 E. 66th Street
Minneapolis, MN 55423

General Council of the Assemblies of God
Deferred Giving and Trusts Dept.
1445 Boonville Avenue
Springfield, MO 65802

Institute for Creation Research
Thomas L. Manning
P.O. Box 2667
El Cajon, CA 92021

Missionary Church
Stewardship Office
3901 S. Wayne Avenue
Ft. Wayne, IN 46807

Moody Bible Institute
Alan B. Terwilleger
820 N. LaSalle Drive
Chicago, IL 60610

Pentecostal Church of God
Office of the General Secretary
P.O. Box 850
Joplin, MO 64802

Wycliffe Bible Translators
Development Department
P.O. Box 2727
Huntington Beach, CA 9264

Non-affiliated groups and denominations that invite your inquiries about programs and services offered.

Church of God World Service
Office of Wills and Estate Planning
P.O. Box 2420
Anderson, IN 46018

Crystal Cathedral Ministries
(The Hour of Power)
Planned Giving Department
12141 Lewis Street
Garden Grove, CA 92640

Lutheran Brotherhood
625 4th Avenue S
Minneapolis, MN 55415

"Offers a broad range of financial products and services to Lutherans nationwide, including life and health insurance, annuities, mutual funds, and other investments. A fraternal benefit society, it aids its members, their communities, and Lutheran institutions through a variety of charitable and benevolent programs and resources."

**National Catholic
Stewardship Council, Inc.**
Matthew R. Paratore
National Director
1275 K Street N.W.
Suite 980
Washington, D.C. 20005

**The Southern Baptist
Convention**
For materials:
SBC Stewardship Services
127 Ninth Avenue, North
Nashville, TN 37234

For specific information:
Stewardship Commission
901 Commerce Street
Suite 650
Nashville, TN 37203

Banking and Savings Programs with Social Mandates

Ameritrust Development Bank
1228 Euclid Avenue
Cleveland, OH 44115
(216) 861-6964

A subsidiary of Ameritrust, the bank has a mission to "provide financial services to low and moderate income communities, corporations, partnerships, and individuals" in the Cleveland area. The bank offers CDs, money market deposits, and savings accounts. Minimum deposit is $500 for most. Deposits are FDIC insured.

The Bridge Fund
ACCION International
130 Prospect Street
Cambridge, MA 02139
(617) 492-4930

When you contract with this fund, the fund purchases a CD at the South Shore or Chemical Bank. The bank issues a letter of credit to several South American and Latin American banks to guarantee loans made to very small businesspersons. Average loan is under $200. The average loan recipient has experienced a 30% increase in income during the first year of the loan. Minimum loan to the fund is $10,000 and for 18 months. Check the 30 November 1987 edition of *Forbes* for an article about this organization's remarkable work.

First American Credit Union
P.O. Box 99
Casa Grande, AZ 85222
(602) 836-1531

First American has assets of $20,000,000 and makes loans to the Indian tribes of the Southwest. Offers money market funds and certificates of deposit. Insurance to $100,000 by the National Credit Union Administration.

Self-Help Credit Union
413 East Chapel Hill Street
Durham, NC 27701
(919) 683-3016

Its goal is to "promote economic development among minorities, women, rural, and low-income people across the state." Offers a variety of accounts at competitive rates for individuals, institutions, and churches. Deposits are insured to $100,000 by the National Credit Union Administration.

South Shore Bank
Joan Shapiro, Vice President
71st and Jeffery Boulevard
Chicago, IL 60649
(312) 288-1000

South Shore is the nation's first and only private neighborhood development bank. It specializes in lending to rebuild deteriorated neighborhoods for low-income and minority residents. The bank offers money market funds, certificates of deposit, IRAs, and other savings beginning at $250. FDIC coverage is provided, and rates are competitive.

Shorebank Advisory Services, Inc.
1950 E. 71st Street
Chicago, IL 60649-2096
(312) 280-4740

An affiliate of South Shore Bank, this service was organized to assist other financial institutions which might be interested in the bank's approach to social banking.

The Vermont National Bank
Socially Responsible Banking Fund
Elizabeth D. Kent, Coordinator
P.O. Box 804
Brattleboro, VT 05301
(802) 257-7151

"The Socially Responsible Banking Fund, established in January of 1988, allows depositors more control over how their funds are invested. SRB funds are targeted to the areas of affordable housing, small business development, education, agriculture, and environmental/conservation concerns in Vermont communities. The fund offers a wide range of deposit accounts with a starting balance of $500. Every depositor is FDIC insured up to $100,000."

Bonds

Some bonds you might consider for a balance of safety and social merit. Please review each thoroughly before investing.

"Fannie Maes" are similar to regular Ginnie Maes, described below. They offer a "moral" guarantee by the federal government, slightly less binding than Ginnie Maes. Therefore, they usually offer slightly higher rates. They are available in 30-year varieties and in 15-year varieties called "Dwarfs."

"Ginnie Maes" essentially route your money to home-buyers who desire a 30-year mortgage. You receive a fixed interest rate, a monthly check of interest and principal, and a guarantee of the US Treasury. Minimum investment is usually quoted at $25,000, but older bonds are available for $10,000 and under. Average life at issue is 12 years.

"Midget Ginnie Maes" essentially route your money to home-buyers who desire a 15-year mortgage. You receive a fixed interest rate, a monthly check of interest and principal, and a guarantee of the US Treasury. Minimum investment approximates $20,000 at this time. Average life at issue is 6 years.

"Mobile Home Ginnie Maes" essentially route your money to those desiring to buy a mobile home. Available in 15-year and 30-year varieties. Average maturities are a little shorter than with other Ginnie Maes. You receive a fixed rate, monthly checks of interest and principal, and a guarantee of the US Treasury. These are sometimes available for about $15,000.

Other agencies you should consider:

Federal Home Loan Mortgage
    Corporation (Freddie Mac's)

Federal Farm Credit Banks

Federal Home Loan Banks

Many mutual funds allow smaller investments into government agency bonds.

Mortgage-backed securities return a part of your principle each month (as discussed in chapter 7). If you would like to lend to those needing a mortgage but want more (though not definite) predictability in the timing of this return of principal, you might consider a "Collateralized Mortgage Obligation" or "CMO." Your broker or banker should have a brochure on the varieties available.

Mutual Funds with Social Criteria

Some funds describe their screening methods in their sales literature and prospectus, while others simply apply screens without identification. Some funds have more restrictive screens than others. Minimum investments are as low as a few hundred dollars.

Some mutual fund groups make special arrangements to manage money for institutional investors such as churches, seminaries, and foundations. Some of the mutual funds listed here also manage money within variable annuities.

American Mutual Fund or,
Washington Mutual
   Investors Fund
American Funds Distributors
333 South Hope Street
Los Angeles, CA 90071

Calvert Securities Corporation
4550 Montgomery Avenue
Suite 1000 North
Bethesda, MD 20814

Dreyfus Third Century Fund
Dreyfus Service Corporation
666 Old Country Road
Garden City, NY 11530

Fidelity Environmental
   Services
P.O. Box 660603
Dallas, TX 75266-0663

Freedom Environmental Fund
Freedom Distributors
   Corporation
One Beacon Street
Boston, MA 02108

Lincoln National Life
   Insurance Company
P.O. Box 1110
Fort Wayne, IN 46801
Attention: Special Annuities
   Markets

They offer a variable annuity with a "Social Awareness Fund" as an option.

Parnassus Fund
244 California Street
San Francisco, CA 94111

Pax World Fund
224 State Street
Portsmouth, NH 03801

Pioneer Group, Inc.
60 State Street
Boston, MA 02109-1975

Scudder, Stevens and Clark
175 Federal Street
Boston, MA 02110-2267

I have a personal regard for the
Scudder group of mutual

funds. While I'm unaware of
ethical screens, they have
demonstrated works in the area
of ethics and investments.

**Templeton Funds
Distributors**
P.O. Box 33030
St. Petersburg, FL 33733-8030

Working Assets Money Fund
230 California Street
Suite 500
San Francisco, CA 94111

Money Management Firms with Social Screening Capabilities

The list of management firms employing screening techniques is
growing daily. Here are some for consideration.

Amy Domini
Loring, Wolcott & Coolidge
 Office
230 Congress Street
Boston, MA 02110
(617) 523-6531

Ms. Domini is the co-author of
Ethical Investing. Loring, Wolcott & Coolidge is a firm of
private professional fiduciaries
for substantial investors. Minimum account size would ap-
proximate $500,000. (I would

like to gratefully acknowledge
the assistance of Ms. Domini in
compiling the banking institutions of this resource center.)

**Capital Guardian Trust
 Company**
John H. Seiter
Senior Vice President
333 South Hope Street
Los Angeles, CA 90071
(213) 486-9200

One of the world's oldest, largest, and most successful management organizations. Minimum domestic account is $20,000,000. Minimum international account would be $10,000,000.

Christian Brothers Investment Services Inc.
245 Park Avenue
10th Floor
New York, NY 10167
(212) 272-6750

Participant base is Catholic institutional investors seeking investment advice or investment vehicles ranging from cash management through long-term funds.

Eagle Investment Associates
(A Division of Bank of Boston)
155 Federal Street
Boston, MA 02110
(617) 434-5706

Eagle offers individualized portfolio management for those with a minimum of $500,000.

Franklin Research & Development Corporation
711 Atlantic Avenue
Boston, MA 02111
(617) 423-6655

Branch offices can be found in Sausalito, California, and Seattle, Washington. An investment advisory firm managing socially responsive investments exclusively. Minimum account is $400,000. They also publish the monthly newsletters "Franklin's Insight" and "Investing for a Better World."

Newbold's Investment Advisors
Brian McGrath
1500 Walnut Street
Philadelphia, PA 19102
(215) 893-8180

An experienced division within an old-line investment firm. Consistently manages in the "value" philosophy. Minimum investment is $500,000.

Scudder, Stevens & Clark
Suanne K. Luhn, Director
600 Vine Street
Suite 2000
Cincinnati, OH 45202-2430
(513) 621-2733

A division of an old line, independent firm offering socially screened portfolios for $3,000,000 minimum.

Stein Roe & Farnham, Inc.
Michael S. Sutton
First Fort Lauderdale Place
100 N.E. 3rd Avenue
Suite 800
Fort Lauderdale, FL
  33301-1146
(305) 764-7800

A major money management firm that offers several screening capabilities. Minimum investment would be approximately $600,000.

Templeton Investment Counsel, Inc.
Jim Wood, Senior Vice President
Broward Financial Centre
Suite 2100
Ft. Lauderdale, FL 33394
(305) 764-7390

A division of John Templeton's organization. Minimum account size is $10,000,000.

**United States Trust
   Company**
Asset Management Division,
   Trust Department
40 Court Street
10th Floor
Boston, MA 12108
(617) 726-7250

U.S. Trust is one of the largest and most experienced managers of broadly based social portfolios. Minimum account size is $1,000,000.

Recommended Reading

All Christian investors should become very familiar with the biblical books of Proverbs, Ecclesiastes, Luke, Acts, and James. For additional insights into Christian principles and the handling of money and investments, the following books may be helpful.

Ethical Investing
Amy L. Domini and Peter D.
   Kinder
Addison-Wesley Publishing
Company, Inc.

A ground-breaking book about the ethics of investing. I would recommend it to a fairly knowledgeable investor or one looking to be more ethical about his or her investing.

---

*Ethics in the Financial
   Marketplace*
John L. Casey
Managing Director
Scudder, Stevens & Clark, Inc.
345 Park Avenue
New York, NY 10154
(212) 326-6200

Should be read by any financial planner, broker, trust manager, or money manager interested in the ethics of his or her profession. A thought-provoking work. I highly recommend it to business school students for its interesting casework.

Faith and $avvy, Too! The Christian Woman's Guide to Money
Judith Briles

Written specifically for women with little financial background, this is a bit more aggressive than most books I've read by Christian financial planners. Gives fairly general investment advice.

———————

The Holy Use of Money
John C. Haughey, S.J.
Doubleday & Company, Inc.

An in-depth look at the theology of handling financial resources. Strongly recommended for church leaders who advise stewardship efforts and invest church funds. No specific investment recommendations are made.

———————

Money & Power
Jacques Ellul
Inter-Varsity Press

A very scholarly examination of the economic, societal, and spiritual problems money can create for Christians.

———————

The Templeton Plan: 21 Steps to Personal Success and Real Happiness
James Ellison
Harper & Row, Publishers

John Templeton's approach to life. I would recommend it to any businessperson or investor seeking guiding principles for everyday life. Firmly grounded in Christian principles. Not an investment book, but compelling.

———————

The Touche Ross Personal Financial Management & Investment Workbook
John R. Connell
Prentice Hall Publishers

A unique workbook by this Big-8 accounting firm. A complete guide to do-it-yourself financial planning. Complete with worksheets and tax-tables. Available at your local bookstore or through the firm's local office. Gives general investment guidance.

———————

Larry Burkett and Ron Blue have written several informative books on Christian principles of handling money and budgeting, and they offer some general investment advice. Ask about their books at your local religious bookstore.

Brochures, Newsletters, and Organizations of Interest

The Clean Yield
Box 1880
Greensboro Bend, VT 05842

A "stock market newsletter for investors who would like to make timely and profitable investments in publicly traded companies that pass certain social responsibility tests." $75 per year for individuals and non-profit groups.

The Corporate Examiner
Interfaith Center on
    Corporate Responsibility
475 Riverside Drive
Room 556
New York, NY 10115

Published ten times a year, this newsletter advises on corporate activities of concern and investments of interest to the ethically aware. Cost is $35 per year.

Ethics in American Business: A Special Report
Deloitte and Touche
1633 Broadway
New York, NY 10019
c/o Cathy Coult

A special report from a national accounting firm on the state of ethics in America. Contains writings by such leaders as Warren Burger, Eric Sevareid, Felix Rohatyn, and Lester Thurow. A must read for any professional in America today.

The Eye of the Needle
120 North Fourth Street
Minneapolis, MN 55401

"A bi-monthly perspective on the responsible use of wealth, power, and position." Written from a Christian perspective. No specific investment advice is given, but a very nicely done publication. $27 per year.

Good Money: The Newsletter for Socially Concerned Investors
Good Money Publications, Inc.
Box 363
Worcester, VT 05682

A bi-monthly publication that provides specific recommendations and information about stocks and mutual funds suitable for the ethically aware. Subscriptions are $75 per year. The organization also provides portfolio screening on a fee basis.

The Investor Responsibility Research Center
1319 F Street NW
Suite 900
Washington, D.C. 20004
(202) 939-6500

Offers a fee-based service to institutional investors. Provides information about proxy matters and other corporate developments. Publishes a newsletter called "News for Investors" about similar issues. Cost is $200 per year.

Managing Our Money: Workbook on Women and Personal Finances
Joyce D. Sohl
c/o The United Methodist Church
475 Riverside Drive
Room 1503
New York, NY 10115

Ms. Sohl is an associate treasurer of the United Methodist Church. This 75-page workbook is an excellent resource for women beginning to manage money. Cost is $4.55.

Mutual Fund Values
Morningstar, Inc.
53 W. Jackson Boulevard
Chicago, IL 60604

An independent analytical service that provides insight into most mutual funds offered in the U.S. A three-month trial subscription is available for $55. An annual subscription is $375.

The Social Investment Forum
711 Atlantic Avenue
Boston, MA 12111

An association of those interested in ethical investing. The Forum publishes a guide of its members that would be of interest to investors seeking products, brokers, and planners. It also publishes a quarterly newsletter for its members. Write for various fees and costs.

Socially Responsible Investing: We Believe You Don't Have to Sacrifice Profits for Principles
Shearson Lehman Hutton
200 Vesey Street
New York, NY 10285-2700
Attention: Janet Coolick

A special report from one of America's largest investment firms.

Thoughtful Investing
The Institute for Thoughtful Investing, Inc.
P.O. Box 3546
Plant City, FL 33564

A bi-monthly newsletter updating those of the Judeo-Christian persuasion about professionals and institutions (both financial and religious) doing interesting work. $29 per year.

The Value Line Investment Survey
711 Third Avenue
New York, NY 10017

An independent company that

researches and makes investment recommendations on about 2000 common stocks. It is updated weekly and costs about $500 a year. Also available in most libraries and investment firms.

Organizations

Kinder, Domini and Company
7a Dana Street
Cambridge, MA 02138

"Does the stock selection for the Domini Social Index Fund. In addition, the firm sells *Corporate Profiles*, a social profile on the largest 1,000 companies based in America. It also offers customized services on a consulting basis."

National Association of Community Development Loan Funds
151 Montague City Road
Greenfield, MA 01301
(413) 774-7956

An association of loan funds in communities denied sufficient access to traditional capital markets. The NACDLF provides information about current funds and technical assistance in starting a fund. Many allow you to set your interest rate from zero to current market rates. They typically address the most

basic needs of the communities they serve. Religious endowment funds and pension funds should give these vehicles particular attention.

National Federation of Community Development Credit Unions
29 John Street
Suite 903
New York, NY 10038
(202) 513-7191

An association of credit unions serving low-income areas. The Federation works to promote neighborhood reinvestment and non-profit consumer financial services in poor neighborhoods.

National Insurance Consumer Organization
121 N. Payne Street
Alexander, VA 22314

NICO publishes various items about saving on insurance costs.

Taskforce on Churches and Corporate Responsibility
129 St. Clair Avenue West
Toronto, Ontario M4V 1M5
(202) 546-6206

An ecumenical organization implementing social responsiblity concepts in Canada.

We have been the recipients of the choicest bounties of heaven; we have been preserved these many years in peace and prosperity; we have grown in numbers, wealth and power as no other nation has ever grown. But we have forgotten God. We have forgotten the gracious hand which preserved us in peace and multiplied and enriched and strengthened us, and we have vainly imagined, in the deceitfulness of our hearts, that all these blessings were produced by some superior wisdom and virtue of our own. Intoxicated with unbroken success we have become too self-sufficient to feel the necessity of redeeming and preserving grace, too proud to pray to the God that made us. It is the duty of nations as well as of men to owe their dependence upon the overruling power of God.

Abraham Lincoln
1863

Resource
Center

And so I tell you: make friends for yourselves with worldly wealth, so that when it gives out, you will be welcomed in the eternal home. Whoever is faithful in small matters will be faithful in large ones; whoever is dishonest in small matters will be dishonest in large ones. If, then, you have not been faithful in handling worldly wealth, how can you be trusted with true wealth?

Jesus of Nazareth
Luke 16:9–11